VOICES OF GRACE

Women Empowering Prayer

Rev. Dr. Julia D. McKinley
Rev. Dr. Mary H. Washam
Pastor Carolyn Duggins
Pastor Arlene Delores Presley
Rev. Gwendolyn E. Wheeler

ISBN: 979-8-9926537-0-0

Publisher: DF Publishing (www.churchgirlceo.org)
Book Cover Design: Brandon Jolly
Editing & Page layout/format: Chelsia McCoy
(www.yourwritingtable.com)

Dedication

To My Beloved Children, Yvette Marie, and Derrick Bernard Blackwell,

This book is a testament to my prayer journey and a tribute to the cherished memories we shared. As I put pen to paper, I am reminded of the unconditional love and joy you brought into my life.

Yvette Marie, your gentle soul and kind heart will forever remain etched in my thoughts. Your unwavering faith in the power of prayer was as inspiring as it was astounding. May this dedication be a reminder of the spiritual connection we always shared.

Derrick Bernard, your infectious laughter and boundless energy filled every room you entered. Your sincere belief in the strength of prayer guided me through the darkest times. This dedication stands as a testament to the bond we will forever hold. Though you are no longer physically present, the love and
memories we forged will forever be woven into the fabric of this book. I hope that through prayer, others will find solace, strength, and the profound love that transcends time and space.

With All My Love,
Mom

Author, Julia McKinley

Acknowledgements

To my Co-Laborer's in Christ

I wanted to take a moment to express my heartfelt appreciation for your unwavering belief in this project and your willingness to be a part of it. Your dedication and commitment have not gone unnoticed, and I am truly grateful for your support.

Your contribution on prayer has been nothing short of remarkable. The words you have shared have the power to touch the hearts of those who read them and bring about life transformational changes. Your insight and wisdom have been invaluable in shaping the impact of this project.

I am inspired by your faith and your passion for making a difference. Thank you for standing beside me in this endeavor and believing in its potential. Together, we can create a lasting impact on the lives of others.

May the impact of your words be etched on the hearts of those who come across them, and may they experience the transformative power of prayer through your writings. Your willingness to share your heart and faith is a testament to your dedication and love for Christ.

Voices of Grace

Once again, thank you for everything you have done and continue to do. Your contribution is invaluable, and I am blessed to have each of you as Co-Laborers in Christ.

With Sincerest Gratitude,
Rev. Julia

Table of Contents

Introduction

In a world filled with noise and distractions, prayer offers a sanctuary of comfort and connection. It is a timeless practice that transcends cultures, religions, and beliefs. Whether whispered in the quiet corners of a sacred space or shouted from the depths of one's soul, prayer has the power to transform lives.

This book explores the profound impact that prayer can have on our spiritual, emotional, and physical well-being. Through personal anecdotes, we will embark on a journey to understand the true essence of prayer.

Prayer is not merely a ritualistic act but an intimate conversation with God. It is a way to express gratitude, seek guidance comfort, and cultivate inner peace. Through prayer, we open ourselves up to the infinite possibilities that lie beyond our limited perceptions.

We will share and explore these five authors' unique approaches in these pages. We will delve into the power of affirmations, meditation, and scriptures as tools to enhance our connection with the divine. We will also explore how prayer can be integrated into our daily lives, transforming ordinary moments into extraordinary encounters with the sacred.

Whether you are a seasoned practitioner or curious about exploring the realm of prayer for the first time, this book aims to provide insights, inspiration, and practical guidance. By delving into the depths of prayer together, we will unlock its transformative potential and experience its profound impact on our lives.

So join us on this journey as we embark on a quest to deepen our understanding of prayer and tap into its boundless power. Let us embrace this sacred practice and discover the miracles that await us when we open our hearts and minds to the divine.

May this book serve as a guiding light, illuminating the path toward a more meaningful and fulfilling connection with the divine through the transformative practice of prayer!

Chapter 1:
The Challenge, Purpose, Power and Victory In Our Prayers

Rev. Dr. Mary H. Washam

I.   From Peace to Chaos
II.   What Is Prayer? Does Prayer Really Work?
III.   Hearing the Voice of God

I. From Peace to Chaos

Wow!!! What a difference a day makes. Dinah Washington a famous singer won a Grammy award in 1998 for this song. I am using this statement as an analogy to share how our day-to-day routine can move from normal to abnormal. Situations in our lives can cause us to move from a moment of peace to a moment of fear, in 2-4 hours. Well let's get started on the journey! This journey begins with a simple question. Are you aware life can simply happen without permission from you? Life can change and alter your entire world taking you from feelings of I am fantastic, everything is great and awesome to a state of Oh my God- what is going on in just 2-4 hours, and guess what everything has turned upside down.

I am a living witness of life happening- my day started out as my normal Monday, as the first workday of the week, I adjusted myself from having the weekend off thought to myself- wow, where did the weekend go? It went too fast. However, it was a great weekend because my son came over and we had a good time together, so much so, he spent the night. The quality time we shared was priceless.

My Monday morning began with my dropping my son off at the subway stop at approximately 8:00am. Okay Hope Christian Academy let's do this I am on my way. I arrived approximately at 8:30am, and began to prepare for my students, I was the principal as well as the instructor for one of the classes, 5th grade. I reached for my glasses so I could renew my lesson plans for the week, when I noticed I didn't have my purse. I immediately went out to my car to pursue it. In my surprise I did not see it.

So instinctively I went to my trunk, and I said to myself, I (don't know why I would have put it there), however, it's got to be there but for whatever reason, it was not there, oh, okay. I guess I laid it down somewhere when I came into the building. I then checked the room thoroughly but did not see my purse. Okay, back out to the car,

I must have looked hurriedly and simply overlooked my purse. Unfortunately, there was no purse in my car. Now a rush of panic, fear, sweat is all happening at the same time. Note: at least 15 minutes has now passed, and all my students have started to look at me and are now asking me "are you okay Dr. Washam", my reply- after all I am the principal, instructor, and adult- yes class everything is okay. However, I began telling myself inwardly- "Don't panic, there has got to be a legitimate reasonable answer for all of this.

I decided to sit for a quick moment so I could think clearly and calm down a bit. I then became strategic and asked one of my instructors to go out and grab my purse from the car. Well needless to say, once again the same answer came forth. I didn't see a purse.

Pardon me... I have to take a pause in my story for a moment. To my readers, would you kindly respond to a few of my questions below?

Please answer these questions as honest as you possibly can.

Have you ever lost anything? Y_ or N_ Explain your answer in detail.

_____

_____

_____

_____

Did you feel guilty about losing that item? Y_ or N_
What emotions were you feeling?

_____

_____

_____

_____

Do you think Dr. Washam should have shared her purse was missing to:
    a. God only
    b. Her staff
    c. Her students
    d. To all the above

Explain your answer. _____

_____

_____

_____

Is it possible to experience fear and faith at the same time?

Y_ or N_

My reply to self again- "Now what?"
- Do I panic?
- Do I simply yell out in frustration?
- Do I simply pray and ask God what I should do?
- Do I tell my staff what's going on?
- Do I cancel my class and try to figure out my next move?

With all these questions rushing in at the same time, I then

started thinking about what is in my purse- Oh Lord!

- The church's receipts from Sunday service
- My wallet with 5 credit cards over $30,000 credit on them
- My personal house keys
- Extra set of care keys
- My check book
- Church check book
- My paycheck from Friday

It's now around 10:00am. OH MY GOD!!! OH MY GOD!!! The church will never believe this is what happened. Oh Lord where on earth could my purse be-what am I going to do? Suddenly, in this 2–4-hour span, I realized I was in the midst of a fiery crisis, a test, a trial, and I had no way out except the Lord help me, and I needed immediate help right away.

Suddenly, without warning I was experiencing inner earth-shaking turmoil. I had feelings of confusion; great uncertainty had surfaced on the inside. I felt like I was on an emotional roller coaster that kept spinning and I couldn't get off. I don't know how I did it, but I told myself you must continue praying. You must maintain your spiritual connection with the God you know in spite of, so, I did.

In that quick moment of prayer the feelings of anger tried to arise and cause my emotions to respond to more doubt, fear, anxiety, and disappointment because I felt God was not listening to my desperate cry to him. Once again, I had to refocus and attempt to stay grounded in my faith, belief, trust and lean not to my own understanding of what I could see which was nothing, but I had to hold on to what the word says which is God does hear and God answers prayers.

I continued to pray this inward prayer, which is known as a consistent prayer, this prayer is a prayer that one renders to God as a means of seeking the Lord with a great sense of desperation about something going on in their life. It is a cry for help. This prayer is a special cry out to God from one that need immediate help from God.

This prayer is one that says "Oh Lord please allow me to find favor in this situation I am in trouble, and I need you, Proverbs 11:27.

This prayer refers to the current anguish and pain I was experiencing but I was unable to express publicly because I was in the midst of my staff and students. The Bible talks about a silent cry. This is when you cry out inwardly believing he does hear you.

Unfortunately, the battle of my faith continued. This whole thing is just crazy, complexed, and just don't make sense. I had to continue feeding my spirit, true faith, trust, dependence in God. I had to surrender my bouts of fear to belief and not allow the unknown current situations, circumstances, or even consequences to destroy my faith in God and prayer.

I had to remain walking in his divine words, his promises, his presence, and his power. I had to remember self-control no matter what and remember He said, "I will never leave you nor forsake you- I am with you" (Psalm 71:14), although there are times when it feels like He is nowhere around!!! The whole truth of this matter was not easy; it was hard. However, the Lord gave me strength to hold on and hold out.

In this prayer I said:

- Lord, I seek relief
- I am in distress Lord
- Lord you delivered Job, Lord deliver me
- Lord help me to contend in my faith
- Lord my faith is weakening; I need help

I had to stay plugged in this consistent prayer inwardly. I had to breathe hard, and grab hold in my unguarded, embedded trust, faith, and renew mind reliance in my heavenly Father God. In spite of what I was truly feeling, which was confusion, frustration, internal tension, stress, guilt, and embarrassment that something like this happened, yet a small voice was telling me to disarm the attack of the evil one-shake myself remain steadfast in whom you serve, whom you trust and believe in. At this point I knew I had to take a step back and ask myself do you really know what prayer is? Do you really believe prayer works? Will you rely on what you know?

II. What Is Prayer?
Does Prayer Really Work?

Rev. Dr. Mary H. Washam

Let's look at Webster's definition of what prayer is: an address (such as a petition) to God; an earnest request or wish; the act or practice of praying to God. (1) Prayer is talking to God. Prayer is developing a fellowship and relationship with God. Prayer is a solemn request for help or an expression of thanks that is addressed to God. Prayer is meant to get one connected with God at all times as one surrender to a state of prayerfulness. Prayer has been designed and ordained to be a point of contact to seek God's favor for our lives, Exodus 32:1.

Prayer allows one to pour out their soul to the Lord in humility, prayer is to cry out to heaven, 2 Chronicles 32:26. Prayer draws one near to God, Psalm 73:28. Prayer is to kneel before the Almighty Father God for guidance, for directions, and instructions, Ephesians 3:14. This is what I so desperately needed. Prayer- is asking God for his wisdom not our wisdom, Romans 11:33-36.

When we pray Jesus, Himself, is indeed touched by our prayers, what we feel, and how our experiences affect our lives. Prayer works most effectively when we welcome more of God's power to flow through our lives as found in Isaiah 55:9-11. Prayer works when we learn how to trust how God chooses to respond to our prayers in spite of what we think or how we feel.

Prayer works when we learn to focus our attention on God instead of the situation. Did you know prayer activates our key brain area? IT'S AMAZING! Prayer draws us to a closer relationship with God as it provides an ongoing connection with Him: John 5:14, 15; James 1:5.

It's quite hard to digest and practice but no matter how God answers our prayers, we are blessed in every conversation we will ever have with our heavenly prayers so, I say to you readers never, ever stop praying!!! WOW! There is power in prayer!!!

The Power of Prayer

Our prayers are God's mercies.
It's like 2 buckets in a well-one ascends and
the other descends.
Arthur Hopkins

Prayer is not monologue, but it is dialogue.
A.W. Tozer

A man is most powerful on his knees.
Martin Luther

God listens to prayer, answers prayer, and He moves in response to prayer. (1 John 5:14-15; Psalm 107:28-36). Persistent, believing prayer is an unstoppable force. This type of prayer is an attitude of the heart. It opens a line of communication which connects with the Almighty Father God.

The use of prayer
Prayer has been:
- ✓ Tested
- ✓ Tried
- ✓ Proven

Prayer has the ability to:
- ✓ Change situations, conditions, and circumstances
- ✓ Change a person's mind, heart, will and soul

Prayer can be in the form of:
- ✓ Audible
- ✓ Silent
- ✓ Private
- ✓ Loud or soft
- ✓ Formal
- ✓ Informal

1. Have you ever experienced hearing the voice of God?

   Y_ or N_

   If yes, explain what it was like.

   _____

   _____

   _____

2. Were you fearful of the voice of God? Y _ or N _
   Explain your answer.

   _____

   _____

   _____

3. Did the voice of God provide any of the following?

    ✓ Instructions

    ✓ Encouragement

    ✓ A Warning

    ✓ A Direct Command

    ✓ A Blessing

Explain in detail.

_____

_____

_____

_____

4. Do you believe God hears us when we pray? Explain your answer.

_____

_____

_____

_____

5. Do you believe God answers all of our prayers?
    Y_ N_ or Don't Know_

Explain your answer.

_____

_____

_____

_____

Some awesome facts about prayer. DID YOU KNOW?
Prayer has:
- No limits
- No Boundaries
- No Restrictions
- No Time Restraints
- No Space Limits
- No Location Restrictions
- No Gender Boundaries
- No Title Restrictions
- No Season Restrictions
- No Education Restrictions
- No Race Limits
- No Spiritual Restrictions

We must never, ever forget prayer is a gift that has been given to every human.

As I looked over the different types of prayers that I mentioned in this chapter: specific prayers, consistent/

persistent prayers, concentrated prayers, and mountain-moving prayers, I am reminded of an awesome story in the word of God about the Apostle Peter. Peter was a faithful disciple of Christ who was imprisoned because of his love, dedication, and witnessing about our Lord and Savior Jesus Christ. As a follower of Jesus, Peter suffered much because of his faith and trust in the Lord. Due to his imprisonment, what did the early church do in the book of Acts?

The answer to that is this: the followers of Jesus, the church, gathered on one accord and purposed in their hearts to pray for the release of their brother, Apostle Peter.

The followers of Christ were engaged in all four prayers that I mentioned above. Their prayers were in total agreement with each other. The mountain-moving prayer was specifically directed to the release of Peter from prison. His release is an ideal example and demonstration of the use of prayer, as well as the display of prayer in action.

When we believe the story of Peter, it shows how we can have complete confidence in the Lord's sovereignty, knowing He is able to do above and exceedingly what is impossible for man to do.

Peter's chains simply fell off as he followed the angel of the Lord out of the prison. What a mighty God we serve!!! Do you believe you can depend on God in the situation you might be in? If so, continue to walk in Jesus' name and watch the chains fall off in your situation.

Peter simply marveled at the power of God as he began to realize what was really happening. He became so excited about his release that he went home to celebrate what Jesus, by way of the Holy Spirit had done. (1Thessalonians 5:16-18). Thank God the church was on its post; they earnestly cried out and prayed to God as they interceded for Peter. Would the church really begin to cry out to the Lord in such a time as this? We, the body of Christ, must begin, and don't stop, don't cease to put everything in God's hands, and be not anxious about anything, (Philippians 4:6).

The early church also began to dig into a mountain-moving prayer. One might ask, "What is a mountain moving prayer?" This is a great question.

As believers who are spirit-filled, walking in power and authority we must learn how to cultivate a prayer life that will indeed move mountains. Church, always remember mountain-moving prayers still work.

LET US NEVER, EVER FORGET mountain-moving prayers started in the beginning in Genesis 4:26. After sin came, people began to call on the name of the Lord in prayer. The people invited God into their dilemma which created the real issue of prayer. Prayers that move mountains consist of:

- Calling out to a God that knows us.
- Crying out to our Abba Father in the midst of our hurt, pain, and brokenness
- Inviting the Holy Spirit to move in our midst.
- Commissioning a divine appointment with our creator Proclaim all of his promises in his God given Word!

Our mountain-moving prayers become activated by faith when we pray to our all-powerful God. Mountain-moving prayers work when we:

- Humble ourselves!
- Pray with passion/fervor!
- Seek God's face!
- Turn from sin (unbelief). Luke 17;6; Matthew 8:26, 27; Mark 11:22-25

This is a prayer I prayed inwardly believing God would hear and answer me: *Lord, Jesus I come to you today as humble as I know how. Lord Jesus, I come to you today to have a serious conversation. I am currently in a 9-1-1 situation right now and it is an emergency. Lord, I need this whole atmosphere and environment to change on my behalf. Lord I am desperate and need your listening ear. Hear my cry oh Lord, have pity on me and deliver me out of my troubles. Thank you, Lord!!!*

Hearing the Voice of God
Prayer Activates the Voice of God!

Approximately 2 ½ hours has passed and I am still without my purse. I don't have a clue what happened to it and I'm simply bewildered and stressed. One minute I feel faithful and hopeful, then the next minute I feel quite defeated and let down that I have not heard from God. *Lord, I need to hear from you Lord, just one word from you will do.*

Suddenly, I heard a small still voice. The Holy Spirit said, "Go back to your car." Well, this was at least the fourth time I had done that, but I obeyed His voice.

A LAPSE IN MY FAITH!

The Holy Spirit said, "Go back to the location where you dropped your son off this morning." I must be honest, I said inwardly, *Are you serious?*

The drop off location was a busy and highly populated section of the city. A quick overview was at least 500 plus people moving about continuously. Many businesses on both sides of the street, two banks, a huge bus depot... get the idea? Regardless of the above information I returned to the scene.

His voice spoke again. "Be still." A good word right? But not so good in the state that I am in right now.

Nonetheless, I obeyed and began to cry out once more in total despair. *Okay Lord, now what?*

Although I attempted to live out this verse -- *Finally my brethren, be strong in the Lord, and in the power of his might.* (Ephesians 6:10-11), the self-talk began again. I found myself shifting back and forth one moment of faith and then one moment of doubt that I would ever recover my purse.

After getting in my car, I drove about five blocks, and this is when I recognized the shift: Self talking- I noticed there was a police car parked that had two officers inside. *Oh great*, I told myself, *since you are a police chaplain in this district you can ask them to drive you to Broad Street and you will get there quicker and not waste any more time.*

Isn't it amazing to find ourselves wrestling not with flesh and blood but against principalities, against powers, against the rulers of the darkness of this world? I was in the midst of a tremendous spiritual battle (Ephesians 6:10). I found myself faced with whose report will I believe, the one from Satan or the one from Abba Father, Our Lord.

The voice of the Lord says, "Did I not speak? Go back to your original location. Did I say stop and get help? Hear ye the voice of the Lord, my sheep know my voice and another they will not follow."

Teach me to do thy will; for thou art my God. Thy spirit is good; lead me into the land of uprightness. (Psalm 143:10 KJV)

For as many as are led by the Spirit of God, they are the sons of God. For ye have not received the spirit of bondage again to fear; but ye have received the Spirit of adoption, whereby we cry, Abba, Father. The Spirit itself beareth witness with our spirit, that we are the children of God. (Romans 8:14-17 KJV)

I need to mention there are many things that are good things, but they are not God things. My idea seemed like a real good, wise, smart and intelligent idea. However, the inward witness was telling me that wasn't what God told you to do; obey the voice of God.

My decision to follow God's voice clearly indicated to me that I was really in an intense battle and the enemy wanted me to forfeit what God had planned. I must confess most of what was going on was far above my head at this point.

All I could think of doing at this point was reflect on the Word of God, which says: Meditate on the Word of God and keep moving. Allow the Holy Spirit to help you recognize God's voice as he speaks His word to you. His word will release every detail for every situation and circumstance in his own time and way. I had to remind myself my ways are not His ways and my thoughts are not His thoughts. (Isaiah 55:8)

I also had to tell myself the more I obey the more I will hear His voice. I realized I could not yield to the flesh which is always self-centered and has an attitude and wants what it wants. I had to continue to surrender my being and be led by the precious Holy Spirit. I had to be a doer of His Word. If I love Him, I will obey Him; I will abide in Him and His Word. I will attend to His message for me: "Go and be still" (Proverbs 4:20, 21); I must allow him to lead me through all kinds of trouble and trust him in the midst of the troubles. (Psalm 91:1-4)

I must always listen to the inward witness, Romans 8:14-15: For as many as are led by the Spirit of God, they are the sons of God. For ye have not received the spirit of bondage again to fear; but ye have received the Spirit of adoption, whereby we cry, Abba, Father. Our inner voice provides supernatural guidance.

THE WONDERS OF OUR LORD AND SAVIOR JESUS CHRIST!

The mere fact that one is able to hear the voice of God simply blows my mind, and to have access to God is simply beyond my little finite mind. To think that we as mortal beings can actually talk to God as well as hear from the almighty God, who is Omniscient, Omnipotent and Omnipresent (Psalm 115:3). It's just so far beyond my small minute comprehension and understanding. I believe and have become 100% plus convinced that we don't pause, or stop to consider nor do we recognize how divinely blessed beyond measure we are as his children .

My prayer is: *Lord, help us to better understand and comprehend what mankind has been given by God, His Son and the Holy Spirit to hear His awesome, holy voice.*

I continued to tell myself, you must continue to pray inward and minister the Word of God to your inner being. Because of my relationship with God, I knew without a doubt prayer does bring one closer to God and this was what I so needed. I needed to stay plugged in every second, so I would not miss God's voice telling me what my next move was. My constant, persistent, and concentrated prayers kept inviting the Holy Spirit in. I continued to seek the Lord for answers that would help bring my feelings and emotions to a place of peace and trust. Amazingly the prayer would always reduce my level of anxiety, which caused me to feel a calmness in my spirit. During this I began to realize more than ever: God does move behind the scenes and moves the scenes that He is behind.

My Purpose and Focus for Writing This Chapter

My focus and purpose for writing this chapter is to challenge every person that will read this book about prayer. I pray after reading this book you will have a newfound belief and faith in the Lord Jesus Christ. He will never disappoint you no matter what it looks like. My God and your God is indeed the God He said He Is!! Revelation 22:13 says: *Omega, the First and the Last, the Beginning and the End. He (God) is a God who is alive today, tomorrow, and yesterday and forever more.*

Let us never ever forget God He is always there for us, Romans 8:37 clearly tells us: *Nay, in all things we (his children), the called-out ones, the born-again believers are more than conquerors through him that loved us!!!* God loves us with an unquenchable, eternal, everlasting love. This love cannot be comprehended with our finite minds for it is just too high for us to even imagine or fathom.

God's love for us is just simply extraordinary, amazing, and overwhelming to us. His great love for us is the reason we have been given the ability to pray and communicate with Him-WOW!! That's totally powerful.

Prayer, yes prayer, is such a mighty, and powerful weapon that has been released at the disposal of every man, women, boy, and girl who loves God and know without a doubt He is Lord. It is truly my desire that after reading this book that your prayer life become stirred, stronger and better.

Amazing News:
TO ALL BELIEVERS...
TO THE PEOPLE OF GOD

As believers, I know you already know this, however, just in case you may be a new believer and you don't know...

Prayer is: A guided missile that can be launched from anywhere on the face of the planet, at any target, and there is absolutely no defense in the entire universe that can come against it. Yes Lord!!

So why is this so important and profound because not even the devil, the adversary, Satan himself is able to stop the power of prayer- Glory!!! As 21st century believers we know one of the prescribed weapons to destroy the acts of Satan is prayer.

Prayer for believers: Help guard our minds and help to keep us focused on our Lord and Savior Jesus Christ Son of the Living God.

In a sermon I listened to, the pastor discussed how prayer lifts us from the natural to the Supernatural. He emphasized how prayer transforms our minds and focuses us on heavenly things above and beyond our limitations.

As soldiers in the army of the Lord, let us learn to roast the enemy with the Lord's authority and power which lives in us, so we will be able to cripple and destroy the strength and power of the evil one. Amen! Amen!

As we sincerely pray the Body of Believers, let us ask the Holy Spirit to activate a new level of prayer and faith to endow and envelope our lives on today and tomorrow for evermore. Yes Lord!!!

My sincere aim in this chapter is to tell you personally never ever give up on God because He won't give up on you EVER!!!

In this chapter my Faith-Trust-Belief was indeed on the line. My faith was being challenged every hour 8:30am-11:30am. My faith was stretched beyond measure. My back was against the wall with the question will you believe or disbelieve what God says?

Once again I had to reflect on what I know at this point: Proverbs 3:5 says: *Trust in the Lord with all thine heart and lean not unto thine own understanding. In all thine ways acknowledge Him, and He shall direct thy path. Glory hallelujah praise ye the Lord.* (KJV)

I had to trust God 100% in order to get the victory He planned in this whole situation. Obedience was to God's plan. I had to consistently obey the voice of God and do what the spirit was leading me to do.

However, I had to stay invested in a Specific prayer, a Constant and Persistent prayer, a Concentrated prayer, as well as a Mountain-Moving prayer. All of these types of prayers mentioned helped me to stay focused and in tune to what God was doing in my life.

The adversary wanted me to believe God did not hear my prayers. He, the enemy, tried to tell me just go ahead and accept defeat:

- Confess your loss.
- Tell your staff
- Count your losses
- Cancel bank account
- Cancel all credit cards
- Contact the leaders of HOPE
- You will never live this down

With all of the above negativity I had to continue to dwell on how good God has always been to me. The popular song came to my mind that reminds us we won't complain because when we look around and reflect, our good days-

outweigh the bad days so we won't complain. Hallelujah! Hallelujah! Hallelujah!!!

How Prayer Impacted My Experience

Prayer became my secret weapon warfare that I use in my challenge of "From Peace to Chaos – From Faith to Fear – From Chaos to Victory. In my spiritual battle, I had to stay focused and concentrate on the fight that was before me. Facing the wiles of the enemy was not so easy, but God was in the battle with me, continued to strengthen me and encourage me. I have read this Scripture hundreds of times before but, this Scripture became so revolutionary for me during my time of testing, Ephesians 6:18. Praying always with all prayer and supplication in the Spirit, and watching thereunto with all perseverance…

It is so vital that I review this time frame, which shows how this entire testimony was all "God fed, and God led." My steps were truly being ordered by the Lord. This teaching taught me do not trace God but TRUST God.

Let's review the time frame in this faith walk situation.

Please answer the following questions.

8:30am-9:30am
1. After the first hour has passed, what would you have done?

_____

_____

_____

_____

_____

9:30am-10:30am
2. Two hours have gone by and still not a clue as to what happened to my purse. Should I give up at this point and accept defeat? What would you do?

_____

_____

_____

_____

_____

10:30 am-11:30 am

3. For real God, go back to the crime scene? It has been over 2 hours. Why would I go back there? What do you think you would have done? Go back or not go back? Explain your answer.

_____

_____

_____

_____

_____

I am truly thankful for my many years of foundational teaching on true faith in God. I will admit even with my knowledge and training in faith, the journey that I encountered in this chapter brought moments of doubt in my life. The experience I encountered brought moments of doubt for me and truly challenged me many times. Yes! That's what I said. Even with all of the titles, certifications, licenses, degrees etc. there were moments of doubt.

What I discussed in this journey was that no matter what experiences I had, ultimately the outcome was that God was going to get the glory out of the situation and others will read about what He, and He alone can do all by

Himself. The encounters in this journey became another catalyst for my growth as it offered an opportunity for me to re-evaluate my beliefs and trust in God that much more.

This journey released a deeper understanding of how having a fellowship and relationship with God is so vital for believers when they are faced with impossible situations that only God Almighty is able to perform. This encounter most definitely forged a more authentic connection with my true faith in and deepened the root in my love for Abba Father.

As I traveled from peace to chaos, I had to embrace mysteries and unanswered questions over and over again for example:

- How could this have happened?
- What was I thinking?
- It's over and done, deal with it.

Statements such as this caused many complexities in my faith. My uncertainties challenged my logic and understanding once again.

When these thoughts came, I had to fight back and give my spirit another boost of faith and truth that God was with me. I continued to tell myself not all questions will be answered and yes, this is easier said than done, yet I managed to do this once again. However, it would really be great if the Lord could enlighten me a little about "where is my purse – and what happened to it?"

Needless to say, The Father, The Son, The Holy Spirit remained silent. How many of you know when God does not want to talk, there is no one anywhere can make him speak – Amen!!!

I had to go back to what I know. It was him and him alone navigating my current challenge-I simply had to be still in my faith and know that he is God. He was allowing my faith to be cultivated as my inner being was being nurtured and strengthened with resilience. My faith needed to be steadfast, unmovable, and unshakable. This journey truly provoked me to confront my:

- Limitations
- Questions
- Assumptions

I found myself in a state where I had absolutely no control of what would happen next. I began to look at my vulnerability vs. my humility. The reality of this became even clearer. Trials and tests do expose one's vulnerability and weakness. In order to digest and absorb the lessons in which I was being exposed to, I had to embrace God's process-not mine.

I must say one of my major frustrations in all of this was God's silence. God simply did not speak for hours. He seemed as though the more I prayed and cried out the more obvious his silence was.

Have you even had a situation or circumstances in which God just would not talk. Email me and share, I would love to hear about it! apolmhw@aol.com

I would like to share a few nuggets as it pertains to our faith:

- Faith has a process, and faith will use a development procedure.
- Difficult trials that challenge one's faith creates personal transformation.
- Faith is not stagnant it simply evolves
- Faith produces resilience to learn, grow, and increase one's spiritually.

I am so grateful to my Heavenly Father for allowing me to take this journey from Peace to Chaos then from Chaos to Victory. This victory became a door of hope in my valley of trouble!!!

My revelation and illumination of this journey was I was actually in the midst of a set up by the Holy Spirit. This set up offered me an opportunity to live out my testimony of faith. My testimony is God is always with me no matter what it looks like.

God was the before the chaos, God was in the chaos, and God was after the chaos. All I had to do was follow his word, believe his word, and obey his word. My task was to continue to pray, be consistent in my prayer, be specific in how I prayed, be intentional and remain in my mountain moving prayer. I had to remember God does answer prayers.

Are you believing God for something that only God can do? Do you need God to remove that mountain by faith and trust in him? Contact me and share. Hide this scripture in your heart. Romans 8:28 And we know that all things work together for good to them that love God, to them who are the called according to his purpose.

THE AMAZING END OF MY JOURNEY

Unfortunately, I must cut my details short because of time and space but I got out of the car as He had instructed and proceeded to cross the street by the subway stop. I walked slowly looking down and around for what, to be honest with you my hopes of finding my purse was at an all-time low.

One thing I need to mention is all of the businesses were now open; actually some of the owners were standing outside in front of their businesses. The banks had opened, the street cleaners had just finished sweeping the streets on both sides. However, I just kept walking, looking, wondering what next. God is with me; He has done miracles in my life-over and over. Somehow God is going to get the glory out of this. God is yet able even if he chooses not to. I will yet love him no matter what the outcome of this is, Amen!!!

If you would like to read this journey in more detail you can find it in my book, "Does God Really Talk?"

Well, back to the end of my journey. Again, I heard the voice of the Lord say, "Stop and look down."
Okay Lord what now?!
WHAT?! OH NO! Just simply couldn't be, NO!!! As I looked down, I noticed two ladies were following me very closely. I bent down quickly and guess what? Guess what was there?

MY PURSE! THERE WAS MY PURSE!

Yes, that's what I said, THERE WAS MY PURSE!!! What was so amazing was the ladies behind me did not see my purse, but I did. But look at the awesomeness of God the Lord allowed branches to land on top of my purse as a means of hiding it.

Can you believe this, though? My purse was actually on the ground wide open. WOW!!! I slowly looked inside-

AND GUESS WHAT, AND GUESS WHAT, AND GUESS WHAT?!
There was absolutely nothing missing!!! Now how awesome
and creative was this? The branches on top of my purse
were a means of hiding it. WOW!
Every item remained in my purse.

Watch this: The ladies asked me, "Did you just find
that purse?" A few of the business owners were still outside
and asked the same question. Well, at this point I really, yes,
really lost it. I yelled, I screamed, I hollered, I jumped up and
down. I cried. I laughed giving my God all the praise, all the
glory, all the honor for what He had done!!!

To everyone that traveled this journey with me take
note. My purse was missing... lost from 8:30am-11:30am
and in the midst of over 500 people coming and going
continuously and no one saw the purse. God dispatched the
branch of the tree to fall down on top of my purse as a
camouflage and dispatched angels to guard it until I
returned. What a mighty God we serve!!!

The God that I serve knew no matter what I had to
face in this test and trial that I would walk by faith and not
allow fear to distract me. I thank God for the strength to
remain in: specific prayer, constant/persistent prayer,
concentrated prayer and mountain-moving prayer. The
Lord heard my voice, my cry, my tears, my fears, my doubts,

and uncertainties, Psalm 116:1-6.

To My Readers:

In this journey, I had to be a DOER of the Word of God. Faith without works is dead. I had to work my faith, not just say it. I had to encourage myself in the Lord it was down to the fact either you believe God, or you don't.

George Mueller quotes: "If you walk with him, and expect help from him, he will never fail you." (2) After reading this I quickly thought about I Samuel 30:6 -- And David was greatly distressed; for the people spake of stoning him, because the soul of all the people was grieved, every man for his sons and for his daughters: but David encouraged himself in the Lord his God. Once again, I had to realize the need for me to think on good over and over again. In order to stay focused, and strengthened, I had to reflect on how God continues to empower me with his purpose and grants me with the perseverance in spite of myself. I continued to assure myself inwardly that God has his hands on my life and:

- Where God guides, He provides
- Whom God appoints, He anoints

The above helped me to recall the memories of God working in my life over and over again. Again, and again this journey put my faith to the test over and over again there would be a lapse in my faith. However, faith would reappear and cause my faith to trust again in the grace and knowledge of my Lord's faithfulness.

Whenever I would go back and forth, it became evident it was because my faith was under siege by the enemy, and the enemy wanted to discourage and frustrate my faith to the point of giving up on God. He wanted me to believe his lies that God does not hear our prayers and He does not answer prayers. But thanks be to God I reached for His Word again! He has:

- Sustaining Peace
- Fortifying Power
- Abundant Grace
- Unfailing Mercy
- Loving Kindness

I would like to leave with you a special note: Thank you for taking this journey with me. Take note how I became engaged, intense, focused and directive in my desperate cry and prayed to God. Note how specific prayers were rendered throughout a time period. These prayers were important to the outcome of my testimony. I prayed a:

Specific Prayer: this prayer gets specific results, (Matthew 20:29-34).

Consistent/Persistent Prayer: this prayer is simply to keep on praying no matter what. Don't let go, don't give up, (Acts 12; Colossians 4:2; Ephesians 6:18).

Concentrated Prayer: this prayer seeks God with all of one's strength. This prayer is intercession for a particular need or desire of the person who is praying. This prayer expects a breakthrough because this prayer is made without ceasing. This prayer is concentrated on results, (Romans 8:28; Philippians 4:6).

Mountain Moving Prayer: this prayer allows one to access divine authority to in their lives to ask what they need, and it will be done. This prayer demonstrates God's ability to be bigger than one's problem, (Mark 11:22, 23; Matthew 17:20).

May God bless you mightily as you continue to pray without ceasing and receiving results!!!

I would love to hear of some of your victory testimonies. Please contact me by phone (215) 688-6012 or email: apolmhw@aol.com

References:
1. Merriam-Webster Dictionary. (2024). Definition of the word "prayer." Retrieved from: https://www.merriam-webster.com/dictionary/prayer

2. Mueller, George. (n.d.). Author Quotes from goodreads. Retrieved from:
https://www.goodreads.com/author/quotes/5825213.George_M_ller #:~:text=Be%20assured%2C%20if%20you%20walk,He%20will%20nev er%20fail%20you.&text=Money%20is%20really%20worth%20no,spent %20for%20the%20Lord's%20service.

Chapter 2:
Call to be Prayer Warriors

Pastor Carolyn Duggins

"If my people, which are called by my name, shall humble themselves, and pray and seek my face, and turn from their wicked ways; then will I hear from heaven, and will forgive their sin, and will heal their land."

(2 Chronicles 7:14)

I believe that God has designed our lives with the most incredible detail. He is intentional in everything that He does.

No one is an accident. He made us in His image with purpose. We were born at the place and time we were as a part of God's infinite plan to do His will on Earth. Psalm 139:14 reminds us that we are made fearfully and wonderfully. Every day, we can seek God's will and move forward to accomplish His plan. Everyone has an assignment from God. Called to be a prayer warrior is one of the most critical assignments for the kingdom of God. Born into a preacher's family who believed in the power of prayer, I often heard 2 Chronicles 7:14 in church. This scripture was written as God's promise to ancient Israel. Questions have been raised about its application for today. It is thought that Christians today can find the appropriate application of the scripture by endeavoring to humble themselves, pray, seek God's face, and turn from wicked ways, trusting that God will hear, forgive, and heal. Other scriptures that I often heard being taught as I was growing up were:

"Men ought always to pray and not to faint." (Luke 18:1)
"Pray without ceasing." (1 Thessalonians 5:17)

These were among many Bible verses that are reminders to pray with the expectation that God would respond to our obedience to His Word and sincere prayer.

The Bible contains thousands of promises from God. Determining the number of promises varies according to different sources and methods used to count. We all have experienced that we sometimes make promises but may not always keep them because we are finite. Indeed, we can always rely on God's promises since his mercy is infinite. Every promise that God has made will be fulfilled. When we pray, we are to pray the promises of God, which will build our faith. Proverbs 18:21 tells us that life and death are in the power of the tongue. When we pray God's Word, we can be assured that we will see God's will on Earth as it is in Heaven. 1 John 5:14-15 tells us that when we pray in His will, He hears us, and if we know that He hears us, we should also know that we will have the answers to our prayers.

As a young child, I remember going to church with my parents. They were members of the Garden of Prayer Church of God in Christ at 29th and Susquehanna Ave, in Philadelphia, PA, under the pastorate of strong prayer warriors, the late Bishop Benjamin H. Dabney and Mother Elizabeth Juanita Dabney. Their ministry of Intercessory Prayer was known all over the world. They ministered to a person's need for total healing through prayer and relying on the promise of God to hear their cry. Often, the church altars were filled with people who came in pursuit of relief from their physical, emotional, or spiritual conditions. They often left the altar wholly healed. Some left their canes and crutches behind at the altar because of God's miracle that had taken place right then and there.

Prayer has always been an essential part of my life. I loved reading my Bible even before I received Christ as my Savior. My father was a preacher all my life. God blessed my parents to become my Pastors at the Garden of Prayer

World's Prayer Center, 2217 N. 29th St., Philadelphia, PA. They were faithful to the call to be prayer warriors. They were "prayer warriors" who were "souled out" and dedicated to a prayer life.

Every morning for 25 years, around 3:00 a.m., they would go to the Garden of Prayer Memorial Center, Philadelphia, to meet God on the church altar at 4:00 a.m. In the evening, they returned to the church at 7:00 p.m. I was inspired by their consistent dedication and perseverance in prayer. I am proud that I witnessed their daily efforts with the Lord at home and in church. Because of their exemplary display of holiness, I learned how to remain steadfast in the work of the Lord. I thank God for their labor and love.

Growing up under their tutelage taught me to pray about everything and trust God for His answer. We saw the results of our parent's prayers. The lessons that our parents gave to my sister and me have been invaluable and proved to provide the strength that we needed. We don't always understand God's plan for our lives. Knowing how to pray and believing God's Word enables you to stand every test.

I developed my enthusiasm for prayer and reading the Word of God as a child. Being a part of a praying family and church taught me the need for prayer and God's Word as the foundation for my life. I developed a spirit of excellence in my desire to walk worthy of God's calling. As outlined in Philippians 3:14, I press toward the higher calling of God, which is in Christ Jesus. I am thankful that I had praying parents and praying grandmothers. Though they have now gone home with the Lord, I've held on to their words and the principles planted in me. On many occasions, I was called to lead prayer or teach God's Word. I am thankful to my parents for allowing me to share my teaching and intercessory prayer gifts. I am blessed to have the great privilege to share some thoughts with you, readers.

What Is Prayer?

For years, the frequent question asked is, "What Is Prayer?" Attempts have been made to give a succinct definition. From the description of prayer, more questions needed to be answered. Why do we pray? How do we pray? Is there a specific posture one must take for prayer? Why do prayers go unanswered? There are uncountable questions to be listed here.

I found no shortage of information about prayer recorded in the Bible. Prayer thoughts are an inexhaustible conversation in churches and in many books and commentaries written to describe and define prayer. We should look at some of the definitions of prayer. Prayer is communicating back to God what He has already said. Do you know that you can remind God of His promises? Let's look at Isaiah 62:6-7 (ESV)

> *v6. On your walls, O Jerusalem, I have set watchmen; all the day and all the night, they shall never be silent. You who put the Lord in remembrance, take no rest,*
>
> *v7. And give him no rest until he establishes Jerusalem and makes it a praise in the Earth.*

So, it's saying that "you who put the Lord in remembrance take no rest." We can hold on to God's promises in His Word and repeat them to Him. We don't remind God of His promises because He doesn't care or has forgotten them. To show Him our persistent faith or belief in His Word, He says we can repeat them when we pray. It is also to get us in alignment with Him. It is not spoken out of arrogance or taking control, but God wants our steadfast faith.

According to the Oxford Dictionary, the definition of prayer is: "a solemn request for help or expression of thanks addressed to God or an object of worship."(1)

According to Merriam-Webster dictionary, prayer is defined as: "An address (such as a petition) to God or a god in word or thought; a set order of words used in praying; the act or practice of praying to God or a god; an earnest request or wish." (2)

The Bible describes prayer as communicating with God, which consists of listening and talking to God. The Bible has many scriptures about prayer and those who pray. The number of times there is mention of prayer and the one praying depends on the version of the Bible.

There are familiar accounts in the Bible that tell us about those who were Prayer Warriors.

1. Hannah (1 Samuel 1: 10)
2. Daniel (9: 3-4)
3. David (2Samuel 24:10; Psalm 4:1)
4. Elijah (1 Kings 18; James 5:17-18)
5. Job (Job 1:5; 42:8)
6. Jesus (Mark 1:35)

Jesus was the greatest prayer warrior. Jesus taught us prayer, but He prayed as well.

I read a quote from R.A. Torrey, pastor and author, which says, "All that God is, and all that God has, is at the disposal of prayer. Prayer can do anything God can do, and as God can do anything, prayer is omnipotent." (3)

Prayer is one of the most powerful weapons one can have in their arsenal. Prayer helps you to heal, changes your outlook on whatever you are going through, and allows you to find peace in your life.

Scriptures have reminders of the importance of prayer. Every believer is commanded to pray to God daily. God invites us to turn to Him in our times of distress, in times of grief, when we need comfort, in times of healing, an expression of gratitude, when things are going well in our lives, and to thank Him for His grace and mercy.

What Does It Mean to Pray Through?
Pastor Carolyn Duggins

Prayer is about praying until you know you have heard from God or a miracle happens. The acronym is **PUSH**, which means **P**ray **U**ntil **S**omething **H**appens. We are invited into His presence at any time and any place. There are those "microwave prayers" or the quick prayers before sleep. They're usually short, quick, and to the point. God wants us to spend time in prayer.

Prayer should focus on seeking God's will and praying until you have touched the heart of God. As a child knows how to reach out to the parents in a way that touches their hearts, we have access to our loving Father who wants the best for us. By design, humankind was created with a spiritual compass that always directs us to God. Our loving Father is closer and forever more loving than our parents – While many of us believe that, *does He not hear us? Or are my prayers not worthy of being listened to?*

As humans, our restlessness and impatience cause us to overlook our God's magnificence and gracious nature. He wants to hear us! He wants us to talk to Him, to tell Him of our worries more often. His munificence knows no bounds, like the parent who wants to give whatever the kid asks but waits a bit longer. Why? Because of the adorability of that request, the look of love when the child asks for something makes them love him/her more every time. That's the very thing you should know about your Lord; He loves us, and I believe He loves us talking to Him about our hardships so much that our prayers are granted with a delay.

You may have heard what has been known as the Pentecostal term "pray through." Some may remember going to the altar and kneeling to pray. The seasoned saints encouraged you to begin to call on Jesus. They would tell you to keep praying and stay out in the presence of the Lord. If you got up too soon, someone would remind you, saying, "Pray through, pray through," and keep calling on Jesus. It was the way to teach the discipline of waiting, which is a part of prayer. After a while, the power of the Holy Ghost began breaking through and changing you on the inside.

Prayer is one of the intimate means by which we can commune and connect to God. People possess basic and everyday needs. Our individual experience in prayer is unique between God and every person. No matter your situation, God has a plan that He wants to give you as you pray.

Reading has become one of the things that I enjoy the most. I discovered several guidebooks written by preachers, educators, motivational speakers, and others about prayer. The Bible does not describe no one right way or general form indicated for prayer. Everyone can talk with God in prayer differently. God will meet us at our point of need. The amazing fact is that the Bible says in 1 Peter 3:12 that the believer has the promise that "...the eyes of the Lord are over the righteous and His ears are open unto their prayers..." What matters most is that we enter His presence, honoring Him in praise and worship.

God loves to hear our compliments. We know the enemy doesn't want us to openly express our confidence in the Lord. Our belief in God is developed when we praise God and begin to pray His Word. The enemy wants to produce doubt and fill us with fear. We know that so many people are struggling to deal with stress and anxiety today. Mental health concerns have become common even in our children. We can make our requests known to God, who can help when we call. When necessary, always seek professional counsel through available resources.

Through praying God's Word, we build our faith. When faith is not growing, our relationship with God is weakened.

"His spirit Word is and life." *(John 6:63)*

"It is living and active." *(Hebrews 4:12)*

It's God's Word that gives the power to our prayers. The good news is that we may all be at a different point in our prayer life, but we can begin reading and studying the Bible and access other Bible study tools.

> *"But without faith, it is impossible to please him: for he that cometh to God must believe that he is and that he is a rewarder of them that diligently seek him."* *(Hebrews 12:6)*

Why Should We Pray?
Pastor Carolyn Duggins

Prayer, that not-so-secret conversation with God, is more than just reciting our wish list. It's like a two-way cosmic telephone line where God takes our prayer life and spins it into the thread of His grand design for Earth. It's as if He weaves the spiritual into the natural fabric in our earthly backyard.

Life, as we know it, is a sensory feast—a five-course meal served up through our senses in this earthly realm. But here's the twist: prayer cracks open a door. It's like God handing us a backstage pass, giving the spirit within us direct access to His Spirit, all thanks to the Jesus connection.

And this is where it gets seriously fascinating. Our obedience, our willingness to move in line with God's rhythm, becomes a kind of celestial dance. God's plans and purposes are this electric current zapping through the heavens, and our 'yes' to His lead plugs that current right into the Earth's power grid. His dreams become our steps, His blueprints our footprints. As Christians, God has given us the gift of connecting with Jesus and the Holy Spirit – via prayers. As Jesus left this world only to return when the time came, it did not mean he left us without a connection – he gave us the Gift of Prayer.

So, imagine that—through prayer, we're not just talking to the clouds; we're bringing down the blueprints of heaven into our earthly landscape. Our voices become more than words; they're the ink on the parchment of God's intentions. And in this beautiful partnership of obedience and faith, we find ourselves not just speaking to the stars but aligning our steps with the steps of the Divine Choreographer Himself. He connects with us, and as we pray, he allows his Divine intentions to flow through unseen barriers and into our lives, setting the stage for everything good.

We often find that the weekly prayer meeting time at church has become the most neglected facet of the worship experience despite the gravity of the conditions we see in the world. The excuse is often that people are just too busy and tired. We need not wait for times of crisis to pray. The Word of God calls for men to always be in prayer and not faint. We cannot afford to become comfortable relying on our own strength. Prayer should not be used only in an emergency. Paul wrote to the church at Thessalonica to "pray without ceasing." (1 Thessalonians 5:17)

In our natural lives, the best way to get to know someone is to spend considerable time in the other individual's presence. Likewise, it is with God. The more time we spend in His presence, the more we develop an intimate bond with Him. Prayer and reading God's Word is how we become conformed to God's image. Prayer should be a priority and as natural as breathing.

When we are focused on God, prayer is not about continually asking God for what we want, but it's time to ask God for His will and what He wants to do through us. The purpose of prayer is God's plan and means to accomplish

His will on Earth.

In Matthew 26:36-56, we see Jesus in the Garden of Gethsemane at a crucial time before He sacrifices His life on the Cross. He took three disciples whom He trusted on that lonely journey. He instructed them to stay while He went yonder to pray. In His instructions, He asked them to remain awake, watch with Him for one hour, and pray. He was preparing them so that they would not fall into temptation. Jesus began agonizing over the events that were about to take place. He began to feel the weight of the responsibility of the task before Him.

Undoubtedly, it was the most significant challenge He had to endure. Jesus was 100 percent God and 100 percent human. It was not about Jesus' human desires then, but He focused His full attention on God's plan. He could prevent crushing events that would come, but the hour had come for which His purpose of coming to Earth in the flesh was being fulfilled. Jesus went to His disciples and had to wake them twice to remind them to pray. Each time He returned to them, they were asleep. Jesus then prayed all night through a place of deep distress until He said, "...Not what I will but what you will." (Mark 14:36 NIV)

Jesus persevered in prayer. What a reminder that God has to be the center of our prayers. How can we lay aside everything to ensure His will is accomplished? When we fully understand and are willing to move outside our comfort zone, prayer will become a joy and not be considered an obligation or burden.

Ever been to a sports game? Or you've caught one on TV. You know what I'm talking about – the place where the noise goes wild, cheers and excitement bounce off the walls like supercharged atoms. It's like when a basketball swooshes into the hoop, a baseball smacks that sweet spot, or a football sail over the goal line – it's not just points but a burst of pure energy, etching memories in fans' minds.

Now, let's switch tracks for a second. Imagine this: God is the real MVP in the game of life. Forget hoops and home runs, He's all about delivering the goods, doing some miraculous healing, and throwing open doors you didn't even know existed. But guess what? He's often that star player we somehow forget to cheer for. Caught up in the whirlwind of everyday life, we overlook His jaw-dropping wonders.

You know that song, "When I think of Jesus's goodness and all He's done for me, my soul can't help but shout: Hallelujah, thank God for saving me"? Well, that's the heart of the matter. Imagine your soul belting out a concert-worthy "woo-hoo" for every healing touch, every door flung open, every blessing raining down like confetti.

So, what keeps us going? Picture this: a mixtape of God's promises on repeat, a highlight reel of His faithfulness. Seriously, think about it – you've got this mental playlist of moments when He showed up, moved mountains, and turned the impossible into "I'm possible." And that's the juice that keeps us charging forward, my friend.

Here's what I've learned through the twists and turns – there's a golden thread weaving through it all. The line shouts, "Hey, God's not just sitting in the nosebleed seats; He's down here, in the arena of life, playing on your team." And when that idea takes root, and you grab onto it like the lifeline it is, you suddenly find the courage to stand tall, believe when it feels impossible, and pray like it's the most natural thing in the world.

So, in this wild ride, we call life, we're not just bystanders but players. And the prize? It's not a trophy you can put on a shelf. It's the thrill of knowing He's right there, leading the way, setting up the plays, and nudging us toward victory. So let your heart become an echo chamber of praise, and let each day be a canvas for miracles.

Are There Different Types Of Prayer?
Pastor Carolyn Duggins

Have you considered the types of prayer recorded in the Bible? Types of prayers include Supplication, Intercession, Faith, and Thanksgiving.

When the disciples saw Jesus go many times to pray with His Father, one day, they asked Him to teach them how to pray. We see His response in St. Matthew 6: 5-15 and St. Luke 11:1-13. This is known as "The Lord's Prayer."

However, the Bible records what has been described as "The Model Prayer," the High Priestly Prayer, or the true "Lord's Prayer in St. John 17. Additionally, it is reported that there are over 650 prayers in the Bible. The number of types of prayer varies because of the different versions of the Bible. An example of a few of the prayers recorded in the Bible include:

1. The Lord's Prayer
2. Samuel's Prayer of Dedication
3. Moses' Prayer for the People
4. Hannah's Prayer for a Son
5. Daniel's Prayer for His People
6. The Shunammite Woman's Prayer for a Son
7. Solomon's Prayer at the Temple Dedication
8. Esther's Plea Before King Xerxes on Behalf of Her People

Corporate prayer, as well as personal prayer, is essential. In the times of corporate prayer, build the unity of the Spirit.

In personal prayer, we acknowledge our dependence on God, our need to apply the Word to stand against the devil's wiles, and praise and worship our omnipotent, omniscient, and omnipresent God.

Why Do We Pray?
Pastor Carolyn Duggins

Mark 11:24: *"Whatsoever ye desire when ye pray, believe that ye receive them, and ye shall have them."*

We pray to make a connection with God. We pray to receive instructions and align our lives with God's Word. Frequently, we ask and expect God to act according to our plans. We are the ones who must come to agreement with His plans. Jesus gave us the example when He cried to His Father, "...nevertheless not my will, but thine, be done." (Luke 22:42)

Prayer may be a hymn, a formal statement, or a

spontaneous utterance of our confidence in God. Prayer may be oral, silent (mental), constant or occasional. Through prayers expressed from the heart, God allows us to express our thoughts, desires, and needs. Prayer time should include the opportunity for us to hear from God. The Holy Ghost intercedes us when we do not know what to pray for as we ought (Romans 8:26).

God's desire is that we worship Him in Spirit and truth. Prayer is where we begin to understand the depth and fullness of God's love. In prayer, God reveals that God sent Jesus, who became sin, the very thing that God hates, that we would be made who God absolutely loves, the image of righteousness. We might ask God to draw us nearer to His bleeding side. God's desire is to meet our needs and answer our prayers. We are to pray to make God's promises available to us.

From the days of Adam and Eve, God has always desired an intimate relationship with His creation. Despite the fall of man, God still values that communication. Prayer was essential to Jesus as He was on Earth. He loved that communication through prayer with His Father. Jesus expressed His confident relationship with God. In scripture, Jesus declared in John 11:42 that He knew His father "always heard "Him. He was motivated to pray because of

His awareness of His purpose in the coming Kingdom of Heaven. This should also be our motivation to pray through our journey on Earth.

One of my favorite hymns that we often sang in worship is "What a Friend We Have in Jesus." We are invited to take everything to God in prayer.

What Should Be the Posture Of Prayer?
Pastor Carolyn Duggins

Though the Bible does not define a particular position in which one is to pray, a short list of scripture references supports various positions, which are the following:

1. "Lying prostrate before God" (Matthew 11:29)
2. "Standing before the Lord" (Genesis 24:12-14, 2 Chronicles 20:5, Luke 18:13)
3. "Sitting before God" (Judges 20:26, 2 Samuel 7:18, Nehemiah 1:4)
4. "Bowing before the Lord" (Exodus 4:31, 34:8, Nehemiah 8:6)
5. "Kneeling before the Lord" (Mark 1:40, Luke 22:41, Acts 7:60, 9:40, 20:36, 21:5)
6. "Placing the head between the knees" (1 Kings 18:42)
7. "Looking Up to Heaven" (Psalm 121:1-2)
8. "Stretching forth the Arms" (1 Timothy 2:1-4, 8)

9. "Leaping for Joy" (Matthew 5:12)

Bowing down and kneeling before God is the most common posture mentioned in the Bible.

Are There Unanswered Prayers?
Pastor Carolyn Duggins

God always responds, and He is always listening to our prayers. Sometimes, the answer to our prayer is not what we want. Occasionally, we are required to wait for God's timing. In Romans 8:28, we read, "And we know that all things work together for good to them that love God, to them who are the called according to His purpose." God's response is always in our best interests.

Why does it sometimes take a long time before God answers prayer? We live in a world where people lack patience. Job's response to waiting teaches us that God has an appointed time for His response. Waiting also requires exercising persistence and endurance. In Luke 11:8, Jesus tells his disciples to pray and be persistent. Our sovereign God can choose to answer our request as soon as the words are released from our mouths. But He can choose to delay or put us in a holding pattern. Persistence in prayer is difficult, but it's worth it. Psalm 55:17 says, "Evening, and morning, and at noon, will I pray, and cry aloud: and He shall hear my voice."

Conclusion

I can say that I have witnessed the power of prayer. I have seen sickness stop its attack on members during church service. God gave evidence of His miracles and wonder-working power through the prayers of the righteous. There have been testimonies of healing from diseases, mental issues, restoration in broken marriages, and other events.

What a privilege I had to read about examples of faith and warriors of prayer in the Bible and witness what blessing can do today. God is still God.

Through prayer, I have come to know the Lord better. In every situation, I found the reality of being able to call on God. I learned how to "pray through, "not only for myself. I was taught to pray for everything, every place, everybody, and everywhere. God has given me the boldness to pray in Intercessory Prayer.

In closing, I suggest everyone hold on to God and never give up. Be persistent in prayer and learn His Word to pray effectively. Do not give in to weariness. Surrendering to exhaustion will bring sure defeat. You may be wondering what your purpose is. We must decide to intentionally pursue God through our prayer life. I encourage you to know that the best is yet to come.

Daniel 11:32 says," The people who know their God shall be strong and carry out great exploits." Daniel knew God; even in adversity, he was strong and courageous. His consistent prayer life allowed him to believe God to bring him through. In these days of perilous times, we can also know the peace of God and accomplish great things through prayer.

References

1. Retrieved from htpps://biblestudytools.com/biblestudy/topical-studies/what-isprayer

2. "Prayer." Merriam-Webster.com Dictionary, Merriam-Webster, https://www.merriam-webster.com/dictionary/prayer. Accessed 22 Mar. 2023.

NIV Reverse Interlinear Bible: English to Hebrew and English to Greek. Copyright © 2019 by Zondervan. Retrieved from https://www.inspiringquotes.notes.us/author

All R. A. TORREY Quotes about "Prayer"
Copyright@ 2023 Inspiring Quotes

Chapter 3:
My Effectiveness in Prayer

Rev. Gwendolyn E. Wheeler

My effectiveness in prayer is based on the scripture in James 5:16b: *"The effectual, fervent prayer of a righteous man availeth much."* Effectual comes from the root word 'effect,' which means a change that results when someone or something is done or happens. The Bible's definition of effectual is producing an effect of the effect desired or intended or having adequate power or force to create the effect. Fervent means having or displaying a passionate, intentional, or marked by great interest in feeling or intensity of feeling.

Whatever is coming against you or in your way, such as sickness, situations, or circumstances, one of the scriptures of effectual or effective praying is found in Acts 12:5. Peter was therefore kept in prison there; this was done by King Herod to vex particular churches (12:1). But prayer was made without ceasing of the church unto God for him. You see, the word without ceasing means a continual, intense prayer was made for Peter without stopping.

We pray, and things don't seem to happen immediately

as we want them to. In 1 Thessalonians 5:17, we are unceasing and persistent in prayer. There is praying, and there is praying.

There is an old song we use to sing, "Don't stop praying for the Lord is nigh. Don't stop praying. He hears your cry, for the Lord has promised his word is true. If you don't stop praying. He'll answer you." (1)

As we read Acts 12:13, God answered the church's prayer when Peter was miraculously released from prison. A damsel named Rhoda heard Peter knocking at the door, but she was so excited to that she ran inside to tell the others without opening the door. They thought she was crazy and said it was an angel, but Peter kept knocking until they finally opened the door and saw him for themselves.

The Bible tells us in Psalms 27:14 to "wait for and expect the Lord; be strong and let your heart take courage; yes, wait for and expect the Lord." As we pray, we need to expect God to answer, no matter how long it takes. We should still be expecting God to answer our prayers. That's the effectiveness that God is looking for us to do as we pray. We have to be effective. The world is looking for us to be effective, and if we're effective in prayer, we will have an answer. Whatever is going on will be taken care of because we believe in God, expecting him to move and looking to him to move with great expectation. Scripture says that all eyes are on us, and the world's eyes are on the Christians. They can't see Jesus; the only Jesus they will see is in us. So, the world is looking. They are expecting the church to move and demonstrate the powers of God. We want to be effective, and we want to be diligent no matter what is going on. The scripture said they were astonished. Believe when you pray like you expect God. God needs to fix your prayer warriors who will not get, will not quit, give up, or stop praying.

However, I believe the word of God says the church began to pray unceasingly. Just as we came together like this church did, think what God would do. This was one church, one body of believers joining in intense prayer. The scripture says one chases a thousand, and two put ten thousand to flight. And knowing it was more than two people praying, see how effective this was when God's people pray.

This is one reason we need to pray. Another reason shows how concerned you are about what is happening around you. What's happening around you with others? What's happening in our schools, cities, state, and country?

Another reason we need to pray effectively as people of God is that God has given us authority over the works of the devil. 1 John 3:8c says, "The reason the Son of God appeared was to destroy the works of the devil."

In another chapter in the Old Testament, the Book of

Esther, a young Jewish girl became queen. She called for prayer and fasting. Some things will not happen except you pray and fast with the needed effectiveness. Her life and her people (the Jews) were at stake. She, her maids, and her uncle Mordecai prayed with fervently and effectively. She had to go before the king, and nobody goes before the king without his permission or him holding out his staff or scepter. She could have been killed going before the king without him calling her, but she said, "If I perish, I perish." But she knew she had to go before the king.

Because she went before the king and talked with him, she invited him and the man who would kill her people, Haman, to dinner. At the dinner table, she began to tell Haman's plots against her people and how he would destroy them. And that's when she revealed who she was.

I'm just letting you know that she had prayer work going on while she was before the king. And that's good because prayer goes where no one else can touch. Proverbs 21:1 says, "The king's heart is in the hand of the Lord. Like the watercourses, he turns it wherever he pleases."

We want to remember that as we pray, we are putting this situation in God's hands. The effectiveness of it will yield a result, and you will get a positive impact when you pray effectively to God.

Reference:

1. Worrell, E.R. (n.d.) Retrieved from:
https://hymnary.org/text/dont_stop_praying_the_lord_is_nigh

Chapter 4:
What Can Hinder Your Prayer?

Rev. Gwendolyn E. Wheeler

Ever thought about what could put a roadblock in your prayers? Here's one: unforgiveness. Yep, it's a choice, a crossroads your will faces. Imagine if, during those brutal moments when Jesus was whipped, spat on, slapped around, He decided not to forgive. Imagine the world then, still lost in darkness.

Isaiah 62 talks about a world blanketed in gross darkness, sin piling up like nobody's business. But here's the twist: when Jesus hung on that cross, battered and bleeding, He said, "Father, forgive them, for they don't know what they're doing." It was His call to make, a choice that turned the tide.

Jesus willingly shouldered His assignment. Why? Because He remembered that showdown in the Garden of Gethsemane. You've got Matthew 26:39 telling you there was a tussle between what He wanted and what God wanted – His will versus God's. And He went with God's plan. "Not my will, but Yours be done," He said.

As us, His people, we've got to get this: vengeance

isn't a cool path. We're faced with choices, just like Jesus was. When we give Jesus the green light to save us, we've also got a choice to forgive or to hold onto grudges. It's a fork in the road. Sins got a price tag, and Jesus foots the bill. That's the deal He struck on that cross.

But here's the bright side: today, you and I can lean on Jesus' words. Check out John 5 – it's like a secret recipe. If we ask for stuff that lines up with His plans, He's all ears. And if He's listening, you bet He's going to make things happen. So, when you're humming a tune, think of this: "Ask the Savior to help you, comfort, strengthen, and keep you." He's got your back, and He's got the melodies of your heart in His hands.

Alright, let's break this down. Jesus? He's got your back, always ready to lend a hand. Remember that verse in Hebrews 13:5 where He's like, "Hey, I'm sticking around. No leaving you high and dry." Jesus isn't just some cosmic cheerleader; He's an active helper. And don't even get me started on Psalm 66:15 – there's a whole playlist of ways He's got your back, just waiting for you to ask.

Ever stop to consider how holding onto grudges can put a hitch in your prayers? It's like trying to drive with the emergency brake on – things just won't move smoothly. Here's the crux: if your heart is a playground for negativity (we call that iniquity – a fancy term for all those ugly things), it's as though you've hung up a "No Entry" sign on your prayer lane. It's not just that God might not be tuning in; you're potentially shutting your channel to the Divine.

And yes, you probably think, "I want to be in the good books with Jesus when this gig on Earth wraps up." To achieve that, you've got to do a bit of emotional spring cleaning. Are you familiar with Jeremiah 17:9? It's a reminder that our hearts can be slippery customers, often deceiving us. Sometimes, the mess in there can mess with your line to God. In your prayer moments, you're asking God to help you clean up shop.

But let's not stop there. Doubt – it's like a sneaky guest that tries to crash your party. You know Hebrews 11:6, right? It's like a sign that says, "No doubters allowed." Faith is the key ingredient, and if you're serving up doubt, it's like a bitter taste spoils the whole dish.

Remember that old hymn, "What a Friend We Have in Jesus?" It's not just a catchy tune; it's a truth that runs deep. Jesus isn't just a casual acquaintance; He's here to take on your baggage – your sins, your worries, all of it. So, don't treat prayer like a drive-thru window. Pray, and then keep the conversation going. Sometimes you'll hear a 'yes' from above, sometimes a 'no,' and sometimes it's more like a "wait and see."

Here's the gem: God's love for you is off the charts. John 3:16 lays it out. Jesus didn't just pop by for a quick visit; He came to shatter the chains of sin, to bring light into the shadows. So, keep your prayer rhythm in check. Disobedience? It's like trying to fill a bucket with holes in it.

Let's talk about Joshua and his famous Battle of Jericho. God handed him a detailed strategy, and Joshua and his crew followed it. The result? Victory. It's a lesson in obedience and how it can clear the path for divine intervention.

If you're up for it, take some time to examine your heart, toss doubt out the window, and dial-up your prayer game. Because when it comes to prayer, you're dialing into a hotline that's always open – a direct line to a friend who's got your back, your front, and everything in between.

In the song, I said Joshua fought the battle of Jericho, and the walls came tumbling down, but what happened the second time? Sin was found in the and when evil comes in, everything has to stop the children.

Israel was defeated by the enemies because one man named Achan sinned. God strictly commanded not to take anything but destroy man, boy, girl, woman, and their King and to destroy the city of Ai. So what had to happen was they had to find where the sin was, who it was that sinned, or what was the sin that God had commanded them not to take. After they discovered who had sinned, they were punished for being stoned.

Achan, his wife, his children, his cattle, and all he owned had to be destroyed. It is terrible to be in the hands of an Angry God or God you disobeyed in the Old Testament. After the sin was dealt with, the children of Israel were Victorious in the battle at AI. Because we are under grace, not under the law, we can go to God and confess our sins, and he's faithful and just to forgive us and cleanse us from all unrighteousness first (John 1:9).

In the Gospel of St. John, specifically John 3:17, we glean a profound insight into the purpose of Christ's advent into the world – not to pass judgment but rather to provide a means of salvation. This encapsulates the heart of divine benevolence.

However, it is imperative to acknowledge that certain factors can impede the efficacy of prayer. Among these, the act of lying emerges as a considerable deterrent. Proverbs 12:22 briefly asserts the divine stance: "Lying lips are an abomination to the Lord." This denotes an unequivocal moral stance against falsehood. It transcends the superficiality of mere words, extending into the very fabric of character and integrity.

Moreover, Exodus 20:16 enunciates a pivotal commandment: "Thou shalt not bear false witness against thy neighbor." The gravity of this injunction is revealed in its context as an ethical foundation for truthful engagement. The commandment's resonance underscores the divine abhorrence for the propagation of deceit and falsehood.

Considering the broader context, John 8:44 explains the profound theological underpinning regarding falsehood and its origin. It ascribes the fatherhood of lies to the malevolent entity often called Satan. This lends the matter a heightened spiritual dimension, rendering lying a manifestation of aligning oneself with that which is antithetical to divine truth.

Proverbs 6:17 underscores the gravity of lying by enumerating it alongside abominations. A lying tongue is depicted as a departure from the virtuous path and an affront to the divine order. It is, therefore, imperative to comprehend the gravity of this transgression, particularly within the framework of a life of faith.

In Revelation 21:8, a solemn declaration is made regarding those excluded from the ultimate heavenly dwelling. Among those mentioned are "all liars." This unequivocally underscores the discordance between falsehood and the divine attributes.

The invocation of Proverbs 12:19 emphasizes the enduring nature of truth and the ephemeral quality of falsehood. This temporal transience of lies serves as a cautionary reminder of their ultimate futility in the grand scheme of divine truth.

Considering Proverbs 26:28, the profound relational impact of lying is unveiled. The metaphorical imagery of a deceitful tongue inflicting wounds upon others is a somber reminder of the profound repercussions that falsehood can engender within human interactions.

For clarity, the veracity of one's words, the integrity of character, and the alignment with divine truth are pivotal considerations within prayer. Lying is antithetical to these principles, impeding the authenticity and efficacy of one's supplications. It is a spiritual and ethical imperative to uphold truthfulness and to remain attuned to the profound implications of falsehood within the spiritual journey.

God hates a liar. The serpent lied to Eve in the garden, saying you will certainly not die (Genesis 3:4). This is how the world became so corrupt by lies and disobedience that will cause you to miss out on your prayer going to God. Don't be a carrier, gossiper, or talebearer (Leviticus, Proverbs 19:11). Do not lie. (Proverbs 12:22) our scriptures that you can read about what it says about liars.

The Lord detests lying lips, and I can give you many more scriptures about a liar. One of the old things the old Saints used to say is to tell the truth and shame the devil; we are people of integrity, truthful, righteous people, and people can see our good works and glory for the Father in Heaven if you find yourself lying confess to Jesus and ask him to help you stop lying and the word says you can ask anything and he will help you.

Another sin that will hinder your prayers to God is bitterness and anger. Hurt leads to bitterness, and unforgiveness leads to bitterness. Ephesians 4:31 says that all bitterness and wrath and anger be put away from you. When we are hurt by someone we trust or are close to, and we don't forget or let it go that brings resentment, anger.. Those feelings begin to grow and develop a root of bitterness which will begin to affect us greatly after a while. That is why if you choose not to forgive, this is the outcome; but if you decide to forgive God will help you to forgive the person that hurt you. Hebrews 12:15 reminds us that the root of bitterness can bring up and cause trouble which may cause many to be defiled. Ephesians 4:31 says to get rid of all bitterness.

Bitterness is also a sin that can destroy life. Romans

12:19 says, "Beloved, never avenge yourselves, but leave the way open for God's wrath; for it is written Vengeance is mine, I will repay," says the Lord." (AMP) He commands us not to seek vengeance but instead to let God avenge the critical elements of bitterness: unresolved anger, the ability to grieve, and a lack of control over unresolved anger. Ephesians 4:6 says that we can be angry but sin not. I encourage you to take time to get into the Word of God as there are many other scriptures on bitterness to give you a clear understanding.

I shared a few topics we must be able to pray and pray through. We cannot let anything keep us from praying effectively, fervently, and intensely. You never know when you or your families or friends need you to pray. It is important for your prayers to be heard.

Chapter 5:
Legacy of prayer

Rev. Dr. Julia D. McKinley

According to the Legacy Law Advisors, "The definition of *legacy* is passed on; but Legacy can take many forms. A Legacy may be of one's faith, ethics, and core values. A Legacy may be monetary or your assets. A Legacy may come from one's character, reputation, and the life you lead – setting an example for others and guiding their futures." (1)

When our life is patterned after Jesus the Christ (Anointed One) and His life of prayer, our lives can effectively encourage others to pray, including family, friends, or anyone affected by this power of prayer, thus leading to a legacy of prayer. Just to broaden our definition of legacy, a legacy is transmitted by or received from an ancestor, predecessor, or the past. The person who begins the legacy must have a zeal for God, a love for Jesus, and lead a righteous life. The life of prayer they possess must be an example to others so that others would follow the example of fervent, continuous prayer.

Prayer and the legacy of worship stem from my grandmother, who birthed prayer into our family. This legacy of prayer is an extraordinary work of grace upon our family line. Many men, women, boys, and girls received blessings from my grandmother, mother, and siblings (aunts), and the results were dramatic. I am a witness that many people were healed, saved, delivered, and set free under the prayer ministry of my family line. Many grandchildren received the "Grace to Pray" and spent much time praying.

We were an "ordinary" family, experiencing "ordinary" life before the unique "Grace to Pray" was given to us. God knew the purpose of our lives even before the very foundation of the world. He knew that Grandmother Susie would be the catalyst for the prayer legacy in her family line. He knew that she would be obedient and answer the call to pray. I am so privileged and honored that God chose Grandmother Susie, my mother, aunts and cousins, me, and my children to carry on the legacy of **Prayer**.

We love to pray. Yes, it is work, but the results of our efforts are worth it all. We are doing the work of Jesus, who showed us how to pray. Let us hear from God, through the Bible, His Holy Word, what He says about prayer. In the book of Matthew, chapter 6, verses 7 through 13, we learn God's way to pray:

7 But when ye pray, use not vain repetitions, as

*the heathen do; for they think that they shall
be heard for their much speaking.*

*8 Be not ye, therefore, like unto them; for your
Father knoweth what things ye require before
ye ask him.*

*9 After this manner, pray ye; our Father which
art in heaven, Hallowed be thy name.*

*10 Thy kingdom come, Thy will be done in
Earth, as in heaven.*

11 Give us this day our daily bread.

*12 And forgive us our debts as we forgive our
debtors.*

*13 And lead us not into temptation, but deliver
us from evil; for thine is the kingdom, power,
and the glory, forever. Amen."*

We have confidence in our prayers because Jesus taught us in the book of John chapter 14, verses 13 and 14: *"And whatsoever ye shall ask in my name, that will I do, that the Father may be glorified in the Son. If ye shall ask anything in my name, I will do it."*

God's word is accurate. God is not a man that He should lie. Therefore, all of God's words are the Truth. His Word causes mankind to transform into new creatures in Christ, Jesus. It is fair to say that God's word changes things. It is even more appropriate to say that God answers prayers. We must believe. We must have faith. It is impossible to please God without faith. Hebrews, chapter 11, verse 6: *"But without faith, it is impossible to please him; for he that cometh to God must believe that he is and that he is a rewarder of them that diligently seek him."*

The diligence of my grandmother and mother praying for the children resulted in us accepting Jesus into our hearts and receiving the gift of salvation. Since my salvation, I believe "The Grace to Pray" rested upon me in a great way. Over time, I developed a love for God and Jesus that would transcend my life forever. I discovered that I couldn't wait to get in the presence of God. I had been taught well by my grandmother and mother how to pray. The more I prayed, the more I wanted to be in His presence; to hear His voice speak to me. I can't describe the feeling I had when I entered His company. I am in awe of Him. I love Him wholeheartedly, mind, body, soul, and spirit. He is the center of my joy and the love of my life. I live and move and have my being in Him. He is the best thing that ever happened to me.

Over the years, I have prayed daily for family, friends, and others as they have requested. I discovered one thing that it is vital to prayer, and that is intimacy with God, which comes from a desire to pray. I expressed earlier that I could not wait to be alone with God, worship Him, and hear from Him about whatever He wanted to share with me. This kind of relationship with God is very intimate. No one shares this time with me and God. Yes, I have become intimate with the God of the Universe, the Creator of Heaven and Earth, the Almighty God. The Great I AM. He resides inside me. Together, we are one. I cherish my relationship with Father God, Jesus, and the Holy Spirit. It's my life.

I would like to talk further about this intimacy I experienced. Developing an intimacy with God happens when a particular time is set aside to be with the true and living God. During this time of connecting with God, the atmosphere must be established through praise and worship. Whatever is not like God cannot stand to be in the atmosphere of praise. Praise will drive away evil spirits and evil attitudes. If you are confused or worried, it will calm you and give you peace. A bible, pen, and journal book are also essential to have with you.

It's also lovely to have worship music playing to soothe the atmosphere. You will sense His presence as you sing before the Lord, thanking Him and praising Him. The Bible tells us that God inhabits the praises of His people (Psalm 22:3). It is here that God is in the midst. He enjoys your fellowship with Him. Eventually, worship happens, and we get deeper into Him, perhaps even moaning and groaning. We enter into a deeper level in the realm of the Spirit. As we quiet down, we can listen to Him speak to us.

Sometimes, God will give us a word through the Bible. He can impress upon our Spirit what He wants us to know. God communicates how He chooses. We must listen and capture what He says in our journal book. In this atmosphere, miracles occur, Word of knowledge, prophecies, and visions happen. We must go with the flow of the Holy Spirit. It is here that we connect with God!

Connecting with God

To truly grasp the essence of connecting with God, consider how you meet someone and instantly hit it off. You exchanged contact details, and eagerly anticipate your upcoming conversation. With each interaction, you look forward to the next, creating a connection cycle. As time progresses, the desire to share in-person moments intensifies. This is a beautiful process of building relationships. The more you learn about someone, the deeper your curiosity grows. Making this connection requires spending time together in person or through calls.

Let's translate this into our connection with God – a divine encounter with the God of Abraham, Isaac, and Jacob, often referred to as the Great **I AM**. Daily contact with God becomes essential, for He is our lifeline. He is the very source of our existence. Stripped of God, our capabilities diminish to nothing. In a way, God is the Vine, and we are the branches. Our sustenance, our very existence, relies on Him. Our Heavenly Father goes beyond being a friend or a giver of gifts – He is our Lifeline, the authentic Vine from which all life originates.

Understanding this concept, branches separated from the Vine wither away. This is a poignant reminder that our connection with the Vine, the God of the Universe – the Great I AM – is fundamental. It's a connection we should yearn for daily. In John 1:4, this scripture reveals that life resides in Him and that life illuminates humanity. This radiance should prompt us to let our light shine before others so they might witness our good deeds and glorify our Heavenly Father. (Matthew 5:14)

Prayer becomes our constant companion, a vital necessity. Remember Luke 18:1? God's instruction resonates: "Men ought always to pray and not to faint." In 1 Thessalonians 5:17, we're encouraged to "pray without ceasing." It's an unceasing dialogue that fuels our relationship with God. Indeed, our intercessory prayers for others find their roots in our connection with Him. As His children, we possess the privilege of approaching His divine throne. We can intercede on behalf of others to lay their needs before Him.

We've been granted access to an extraordinary promise through our acceptance of Jesus Christ as our Lord and Savior. His Father in Heaven fulfills anything we ask in Jesus' name. Thus, the onus is on us to nurture our relationship with Jesus, the Church's Head. This connection, this lifeline, forms the bedrock of our faith journey.

Legacy of Prayer-

As far as I can remember, our family has prayed. As I stated previously, it started with my grandmother, Susie, who gave birth to prayer in our family. This caused me to think about Apostle Timothy in the scripture. Apostle Paul reminded him in 2 Timothy 1:5, "When I call to remembrance the unfeigned faith that dwelt first in your grandmother Lois and your mother Eunice; and I am persuaded that is in you also." That is how it was in my family. God shows us that anyone can be used for his purpose. He chose Lois and Eunice back then, and they influenced Timothy, who became a great evangelist/leader of the Church of Jesus Christ.

God chose Grandma Susie, my mother, and Aunt Mary, who became great prayer warriors and intercessors and influenced me to do the same. Today, as a prayer intercessor, I stand before you, interceding on behalf of others. I continually witness excellent prayer outcomes. Grandmother Susie had little worldly possessions but a prosperous relationship with God the Father through Jesus, His Son. It was no wonder that her prayers were answered, and miracles, signs, and wonders followed her. This gift can be yours for the asking. God will give you "Special Grace to Pray" and answer those petitions and intercessions. Just be available and have the desire to pray.

Grandmother Susie was born in the State of Georgia when times were hard. She married young and had several children. Eventually, Grandmother Susie became separated from her husband and had to raise her children without the help of her husband. It wasn't easy being a single parent. Things got tough for her during those times. But it was in those tough times that she called upon Jesus, and her life changed. She developed an intimate relationship with God. She learned to talk with God. He became her constant companion. My grandmother got into the consistency of prayer and prayed for her children until prayer was birthed in all her children, including Annie, my mother, my Aunt Sarah, and Aunt Nell. My aunts became great prayer warriors and intercessors, praying for many and seeing God move tremendously.

My Aunt Mary was renowned in our family, often

compared to Sojourner Truth. She embraced the Lord and cultivated a deep bond with the Father through Jesus, the Son. Aunt Mary initiated a powerful prayer ministry and achieved numerous victories in her intercessions. I distinctly remember her sharing how she prayed for one of my mother's children to be saved. Remarkably, I embraced Jesus in 1976 as a direct result of her prayer. In 1995, a profound yearning awakened within me to intercede for others. Thus, I embarked on my prayer journey, deepening my love for communing with God.

The legacy of prayer in our family lineage is evident today. It began with my Grandmother Susie, passed on to my mother and her siblings, and continues with me and my cousins. What an extraordinary heritage we possess! Our family's rich history of prayers spans across generations, from Grandmother Susie to her children and from her children to future generations. The mantle of intercessory prayer remains a constant in our lives.

Lifestyle of Prayer

Grandmother Susie's relationship with Jesus became a lifestyle of intimacy, meeting with Him daily. She was always talking about God, her love for God, and the holiness of God. Of course, as a child, I didn't understand what was happening with her. I thought something was wrong with her, but as I matured, I understood. I am reminded of the scripture that says, "When I was a child, I spoke as a child, I understood as a child, I thought as a child; but when I became an adult, I put away childish things." (1 Corinthians 13:11).

As I said before, I didn't understand what was going on with my grandmother then, but now I do because I, too, have an intimate relationship with the Lord. Daily, I meet with Him in prayer; it's a sacred time and communion with Him. Now, I am calling as many people as possible to a time of intimacy, prayer, and communion. I also teach my grandchildren to connect with Jesus daily to fall in love with Him.

Faith in God and His Word will be what we need to be effective in prayer, producing the desired result. Also, I think my grandmother had a unique work of grace in her life to get the prayer result that she did. That grace passed on to the entire family, so I call it my spiritual "legacy of prayer."

Let Us Pray

If my people who are called by my name, shall humble themselves and pray, and seek my face, and turn from their wicked ways, then will I hear from heaven, and will heal their land" (2 Chronicles 7:14). This verse says that if we, the church, would humble ourselves, pray, seek His face, and turn from our wicked ways, then heaven will respond and heal our land. Our land needs healing – I am sure we can all agree on that account. I am sure we can also agree that God is the only way our land can be healed, and if we do what He has prescribed, then His Heavenly Father will heal our land.

Here, we see we can petition God in prayer and follow His instruction so that our prayers be answered. One of the prayers is to petition the Lord of the Harvest to send laborers across the path of those who have never experienced the love of God nor accepted Jesus. Then, those people can invite Him in their hearts and receive the gift of Salvation. This is real and true love. Mankind cannot give you that love because it only comes from God. Everyone needs to experience the love of God. I want to encourage the church (people called by God's name) to pray and seek his face, turn from the present wickedness, and call upon His name. People of God expect God to move in the situation and heal our land!

There is a clarion call to come together and pray. As we agree in prayer, we ask God to move to the cities with the highest crime rate. We call for revival to break out in the streets and touch the hearts of the backsliders. We ask God to save the lost, awaken the world, and pour life into the church. It shall come to pass. Life shall be restored, and the lifeline between God and mankind shall be repaired.

Legacy of Prayer

I spent time developing my relationship with God. He was always there for me. I had to learn to trust Him with every aspect of my life, which took time. After a while, I realized that I could connect and speak with the true and living God and trust Him with everything. After all, He is the Creator of Heaven and Earth, the Almighty God, the Great I AM. I also came to realize that He can do anything but fail. God is Sovereign, which means He has absolute power. He allowed us to choose to connect with Him, the Sovereign Ruler of the Universe, or not. I made the choice to communicate with Him. It is undoubtedly a privilege and honor to have an opportunity to speak with God in prayer. He knows our heart. Since God put purpose in me, He knows whether I will accomplish this purpose.

The prayer mantle that was in Grandma Susie's life also rests on me. I am fully persuaded that the mantle of prayer has been passed to my son, Bobby Jr., and my grandchildren, Bobby III and Christopher. They pray every day and are busy developing their relationship with God. Dear reader, I am also convinced you will achieve whatever

He has placed in your heart.

Prayer is our legacy. Our faith in God and His Word allows us to have the confidence to believe God *through* His Word. Scripture tells us, "And this is the confidence that we have in Him that if we ask anything, according to His will, He heareth us, and if we know that He hears us, whatsoever we ask, we know that we have the petition that we desired of Him." (1 John 5:14-15) God's Word says, "We have the petition that we ask." You must ask. That is key! We can have confidence in God. As we pray to Him, it's important to have faith to believe that God will answer your prayer and keep His word. All His promises are yea and Amen. When we walk the love walk, there is no reason why our prayers cannot or will not be answered.

Building My Relationship with The Father

There is no magic formula for connecting with God. Come with a pure heart and follow His Word to His Throne Room. Psalm 100:4 clearly tells us how to enter into God's Presence: "***Enter into his gates*** *with thanksgiving, and **into his*** *courts with praise be thankful unto him, and bless **his** name.*" I want to share how I spend my time in personal prayer.

I like to prepare my space, making sure I have worship music playing in the background and my bible, pen, and journal book close by to capture what God is saying during our time together. I always ask God to forgive me and cleanse me from all unrighteousness so I can have a pure heart and a clean slate before The Most High God. After ensuring the atmosphere is free from evil or wickedness, I apply the Blood of Jesus and make declarations according to the Word of God. This gets me into the attitude of prayer in a peaceful environment.

Thanking God is very important. I thank Him for all He has done, for allowing me another day, and all the other things I am so grateful for. This helps me enter His gates. Thanksgiving always leads me to praise God and to give Him all the glory. I tell Him how much I love Him, who He is to me, and what He does for me. He is the Center of my joy. He is my All in All, and I want Him to know that. Praising God eventually transitions into worship, a more solemn and profound time with God. However long it takes, I take the time. I don't want to grieve the Holy Spirit. I don't want to miss my chance to get into the heavens with Our God. Once in the throne room, I can make my petitions known to God.

When I have done that, I wait for God to answer. You can say we are having a conversation. The conversation is not one-sided at all. I talk. God talks. I read my Bible where the Holy Spirit directs me. I capture all that I can in my journal. I want to review what God says to me in my quiet time. These times with God are so excellent and glorious. I desire that all believers have this type of relationship with Him. If you were to listen in to my time with the Lord, this is what you might hear:

- "Lord, I adore You." "
- "I honor you and give you praise."
- "Thank you for the Blood of Jesus."
- "You are the Center of my Joy."
- "You are the Great I AM."
- "Lord, I love You and need You so desperately."
- "Lord, I lift Your name on High."
- "Thank you for loving me."

You may even see me weeping before the Lord because His presence is fantastic. Or you may find me writing diligently in my journal, capturing God's Words, whether from the Bible, an unction, or an impression He may give me. I have observed that you cannot box God in. Each session in His presence can or will be different. Our only expectation should be that God will show up. Meeting daily with Jesus is significant to me. It is my lifeline, and it has become my lifestyle.

I look forward to meeting with Jesus, being in His presence, worshipping Him, and listening as He speaks. I call this "Building my Relationship with the Father."

Types of Prayers

The Bible tells us that there are various types of prayers. I want to expound on just a few of them because you will want to utilize them for multiple things in your life:

1. Prayer of Agreement

A. Matthew 18:19 says, "Again, I say unto you, that if two of you shall agree on earth as touching anything that they shall ask, it shall be done for them of my Father which is in heaven." (KJV)

If you can get an agreement partner to have the same opinion about what you are praying for, scripture teaches us that it shall be done for them of my Father. There are other ways one can use the prayer of agreement. If someone asks you to pray for them for healing, or whatever, you need to ask what scripture you believe we can agree on, and you agree with them. You can harmonize and make a symphony together in this prayer of agreement.

2. The Prayer of Binding and Loosing

A. Matthew 18:18 says, "Verily I say unto you, Whatsoever ye shall bind on earth shall be bound in heaven: and whatsoever ye shall loose on earth shall be loosed in heaven." (KJV)

Jesus said, "Whatever you forbid and declare to be improper and unlawful on earth must be what is already forbidden in heaven, and whatever you permit and declare proper and lawful on earth must be what is already permitted in heaven."

3. Intercessory Prayer

A. James 5:16 says, "The apostle James says, confess your slips, your false steps, your offenses, your sins, and pray for one another that you may be healed and restored."

4. Prayer and Supplication

A. Philippians 4:6 says, "Be careful for nothing; but in everything by prayer and supplication with thanksgiving let your requests be made known unto God."

Don't fret or have any anxiety about anything, but in every circumstance and in everything, by prayer and petition, definite request with thanksgiving, continue to make your wants known to God.

5. Spirit-Directed Prayers

A. 1 Corinthians 14:13-14 says, "Wherefore let him that speaketh in an unknown tongue pray that he may interpret. If I pray in an unknown tongue, my spirit prayeth, but my understanding is unfruitful." (KJV)

Scripture teaches us to pray with our spirit by the Holy Spirit. When praying by the

Holy Spirit's direction, you speak directly to the Father through Jesus, His Son.

In conclusion, intimacy in prayer is where we want to be in Him. To get there, you must accept Jesus into your heart and receive the unique gift of Salvation. All this prepares you to come before the Lord in Spirit and Truth, now you are ready to go before God. With our spiritual atmosphere meticulously cultivated, we stand ready to enter God's presence. Patiently this moment, for it ushers you into a realm beyond the tangible, where a profound dialogue between you and your Creator unfolds.

In this space, words transcend earthly limits, and a soulful symphony takes shape—an exchange so deep that only you and your Heavenly Father engage in it. This is no mere supplication; it's a transformation into an intercessor, crafting prayers that become lifelines for others.

Witness faith's unfold, adorned with miracles defying reason, signs affirming His presence, and wonders showcasing His boundless power. A steadfast belief becomes a channel for answered prayers; the healing touch you extend frees souls ensnared by affliction.

Behold a transformed world—one soul at a time—woven through Christ's redeeming love. Each whispered prayer becomes a beacon, guiding lost spirits back to the Divine fold. Mountains, once insurmountable, now crumble before your resolute faith, tapping into an inner strength surpassing earthly measure.

As you conclude each prayerful communion, remember this isn't a finale; it's a continuation of the journey. Through each prayer, you delve deeper into God's heart, uncovering His plan for you and the world. Your faith evolves into a force beyond limitations, breathing life into the concept of the impossible.

As you navigate this pilgrimage of faith, know that the intimacy nurtured in prayer guides you. With Jesus as your constant companion, your prayers ascend like fragrant offerings. Miracles that follow are a testimony to a listening God, an interceding Savior, and an empowering Spirit. In this divine embrace, remember you are an instrument of grace, a vessel through which the miraculous unfolds, a testament to unwavering faith in alignment with the Creator's will.

I send peace and blessings in your quest for a strong and beautiful relationship with Father God in heaven. To God be the Glory!

Reference

1. Legacy Law, LLC. "What Is A Legacy?" (2024). Retrieved from: https://www.legacylawadvisors.com

Chapter 6:
Prayers for Everyday Life

Pastor Arlene Delores Presley

Prayer of Thanksgiving
Father God, maker of heaven and earth, how can we communicate to you; the gratitude we feel for your loving kindness. We know that you are Omniscient and therefore you know the gratefulness that lies within me!

I am grateful that I serve the Great.

Black Men
Father, I come today on behalf of Black Men. Genesis states that you took man from the dust of the earth.

Seeing, knowing what would take place before the foundation of the world, you know all men.

We pray father that the eyes of their understanding be opened regarding themselves. Colossians1:9 says: *For this cause we also since the day we heard it, do not cease to pray for you, and to desire that ye might be filled with the knowledge of his will in all wisdom and spiritual understanding.*

God Cares... Death of a Father
The Eternal GOD is thy refuge, underneath are His everlasting arms. Matthew 5:6 Blessed are they that mourn for they shall be comforted. Happy are they that mourn for comfort is there. For years your father and you have had a bond. He was your protector. As we think on that relationship, I am reminded of another FATHER.

A FATHER that also wants a close relationship with His Children.

A FATHER that desires the best for them.

A FATHER that loves us so much, HE gave His son for them.

Through one man sin came into the world, which separated us from GOD.

Through one man salvation came into the world reconciling, us back to GOD.

But there is a condition: We must accept that Gift on a personal level.

That Gift is JESUS John 3:16.

Life
The beauty of life can't be known.
Our Father has shown.
That in Him we have this
Marvelous Treasure

Friends

Father, I thank you for allowing my
Friend to be my friend...
Before they left this earth

Darkness

God, it's dark now.
With you it does get brighter
And brighter

LORD, we come before you in the precious name above all names, JESUS, through the power of the Holy Ghost.

Using the authority that you have endowed every born-again believer with. We speak to principalities and powers, rulers of darkness that bring and have brought darkness to this divinely orchestrated universe. They have blinded people for centuries. We bind their work and the work that has transferred and continues to transfer from the very beginning. That work in the city and the state and these great United States. Father, we walk in oneness with you, and that oneness has the wherewith to invoke change. Genesis 1:31a and God saw everything that He had made, and, behold, it was very good. The earth created by GOD for His glory...

The beauty of this land for HIS creation to enjoy.

We will not allow Satan to come and disrupt and destroy

As he has tried to do since creation!

Amen.

Generations

Heavenly Father, according to scripture, "The earth is yours and everything in it. As a family, as far back as I can remember our lives have been a struggle, UP and DOWN. Sometimes money and sometimes not. According to Proverbs 13:22a, A good man leaves an inheritance to his children's children.

Proverbs 10:22 states that the blessing of the LORD, It maketh rich, and he addeth no sorrow with it. Our generation and future that have prepared themselves, I may not see it in my life time, but I'd like to know that YOU have opened a door for members of my family that have prepared themselves to go through.

You have opened their eyes and ears, to work together in unity, every wife in her perspective place, every husband in his place, operating in the laws you have set forth, with respect and honor toward one another.

We'd like to leave wealth for the next Generation.

Our position is to be the Head and not the TAIL.

A family of LEADERS, A family of LENDERS and not BORROWERS.

FATHER, we ask that barriers that have been erected for years come down!

We have because we ask not! We aren't asking AMISS to heap on ourselves.

We're asking for our family members to sit in another position in this life and for Generations to come!

Thank You

FATHER, we come today in JESUS' name thanking you for FAMILY.

We know that there are times when for one reason or another the ties of family are broken, a mother/father dies, leaves the home or just isn't there in the raising of the children, in nurturing of the wife, a helpmeet to the husband.

We present these homes to you, give the leaders there, wisdom, knowledge, for we know that many of them don't know that YOU are the answer.

Holy Spirit, lead them in the way they should go.

Touch my father, mother, sister, brother, and friend.

James said it; James 1:5, If any of you lacks wisdom, he should ask God, who gives generously to all without finding fault, and it will be given to him. (NIV)

LORD, It's five minutes to midnight
But, I trust the Light that you promised
To those that walk upright...
If there was ever a time I needed you, it's Now.
If there was ever a time I felt close to you, it's Now.
Knowing from times gone by,
that you aren't a man that you should lie.
You'll bring me out of this As I trust and believe...
As I know in my soul...
As the days of old...
You are a faithful Father, this I know right WELL.

PSALM 91

Let me dwell there God...
When I want to give up on life,
with it's evil and much strife..
Let me hide in the One who created me for a purpose.
Let me remind myself of the beauty grace, tranquility
that is found in that Secret place.

ONCE MORE

As you sing to me, A lullaby of LOVE...
YOUR presence I feel even from above.
Now I can step with steps of peace,
With hands stretched to my SAVIOUR I'll meet.

On that day You'll welcome me home.

THE GARDEN
WHEN I come to the Garden
MY Savior is there...
OH! My Savior so precious and near
He hears my prayers
He knows my fears
OH! Precious Savior so attentive and NEAR!

IN THE MORNING
In the morning will I rise, it's quiet and clear
In the morning when I rise, my LORD to hear
My direction for the day, the instructions I find
Emmanuel, God among us
Emmanuel, Emmanuel in thee is my trust!

About the Authors

Rev. Dr. Julia D. McKinley

Rev. Dr. Julia D. McKinley served as an extraordinary Pastor Emeritus in an urban area for 36 years. Her unwavering dedication and profound impact on the community were truly remarkable. Rev. McKinley's ministry was characterized by compassion and steadfast faith. Throughout her tenure, she led the congregation in countless initiatives, including outreach programs to combat addiction, teaching biblical principles in men's prisons, providing care packages to people experiencing homelessness, and distributing warm blankets to those in need throughout Philadelphia.

The warm blanket ministry originated from a heartfelt encounter when Rev. McKinley encountered a homeless man sleeping on a grate while commuting to work at the University of Pennsylvania as a professional nurse in the early 90s. This encounter spurred her into action, igniting her passion to make a difference.

Not only did Rev. McKinley spearhead outreach efforts, but she also collaborated with the fire department to distribute fire alarms in local neighborhoods. Additionally, she spread over 100,000 tracts entitled "You are Loved" in the Oak Lane section of Philadelphia and the city badlands known for their challenges and struggles.

Rev. McKinley's impact went far beyond the walls of the church. She was involved in the American Heart Association, Girl Scouts, youth ministries, and social justice advocacy. Her leadership transformed the congregation, fostering spiritual growth and unity. Her heart for the urban community was evident as she tirelessly worked to address pressing social issues such as poverty, homelessness, domestic violence, and racial inequality.

Her sermons were nothing short of inspiring, emphasizing the essence of love, grace, and the Gospel's transformative power. Rev. McKinley's legacy as a Pastor

Emeritus is imprinted not only on the hearts and minds of the congregation but also on the entire urban area. Her unwavering dedication, humility, and commitment are a profound inspiration to all who have known her.

Rev. Dr. Julia D. McKinley's remarkable contributions have been recognized and honored with numerous awards and citations from city officials, including which confer certificates on ng named Business Woman of the Year. Her impact on the community and her lasting legacy continues.

NBBI- Education started in 2001- which confers certificates in Seminar, also the backbone of her ministry in the late 80s.

The Challenge, Purpose, Power &
Victory In Our Prayers

Pastor Arlene Delores Presley

Arlene Delores Presley is the wife of Mr. Robert Earl Presley, She is the mother of two sons and the grandmother of four. Arlene was born and raised in Philadelphia, PA. She invited Christ into her heart in 1983. "The desire of my heart is to see men built up in God, and take their place in their homes, in this city, in this state, and in this nation. No longer enslaved by the bottle, needle, men, women or any other vice that would bind them."

Life Scripture... (Psalms 34:19) Many are the afflictions of the righteous: but the Lord delivers him out of them all.

Thanks be to God!

Pastor Carolyn Duggins

Pastor Carolyn Duggins is a Pastor, Evangelist, singer, teacher, and author. She is Pastor of Garden of Prayer Memorial Center in Philadelphia, PA, which was founded by her parents, the late Elder William Duggins, and the late Mother Annie L. Duggins. She also currently serves as a co-pastor on the Pastoral Council of Kingdom Empowerment Ministries, Philadelphia, PA.

Pastor Carolyn Duggins is a native of Philadelphia, PA. She is the younger of two children. Her parents' tenacity in leading prayer at the church at 4:00AM and 7:00 PM daily, became the model she followed. She grew up with a passion for ministry and prayer. She learned from both of her parents, who were her pastors. She values the close-knit bond that she shared with her late parents, her late sister,

Wilhelmina, and with her nephew Tracey W. Duggins. She and her sister had a love for music and often sang in choirs as well as singing a Capella together throughout the city at various churches.

Pastor Carolyn Duggins graduated from Frankford High School Philadelphia, PA. She attended Temple University in Philadelphia, PA for one year. While working during the day, she attended college for 10 years in the evening. She earned and received her B.S. Degree in Elementary Education from St. Joseph's College on May 11, 1975. She received her Evangelical Teacher Training Certification from Manna Bible Institute where she excelled to graduate with the highest Academic Achievement Award of her class on May 28,1976. She retired from the Department of Public Welfare after 40 years and 4 months of employment.

Her spiritual journey began in Garden of Prayer Church, Philadelphia, PA under the pastorate of the late Bishop Benjamin H. Dabney and the late Mother Elizabeth Juanita Dabney. She was saved and filled with the Holy Ghost at age 19, at the Garden of Prayer World's Prayer Center (GOPWPC) Philadelphia, PA, under the late Mother Elizabeth J. Dabney.

She served under the pastorate of her parents at the Garden of Prayer World's Prayer Center and then at Garden of Prayer Memorial Center in Philadelphia, PA. She was licensed as an Evangelist in January 1970, in the Church of God in Christ Eastern Jurisdiction of PA. Pastor Carolyn Duggins was licensed as the Assistant Pastor of Garden of Prayer Memorial Center by Bishop O. T. Jones Sr of COGIC on May 10, 1995. She received the mantle and has been the Pastor of Garden of Prayer Memorial Center since June 2003. She continues to have a deep affection to move forward in ministry after her parents passing.

She was taught Old Testament Studies at Charles Harrison Mason Bible College in Philadelphia, PA. Her ministry includes Evangelism Ministry, Noon Day Prayer Ministry, 24/7 Intercessory Prayer Ministry, Morning Devotions Ministry, Bible Study, VBS, Choir Ministry, and Sunday School Superintendent/teacher. Annually, she also serves the community through Skilton House Ministries Operation Brotherhood. She has been blessed to be on the Board and as the secretary of Naomi Ruth Girls Ministry.

Pastor Carolyn Duggins has an enthusiasm for writing Christian poetry. She has authored forty-five poems and a book to honor the legacy of her parents that are yet to be published.

The Challenge, Purpose, Power & Victory In Our Prayers

Pastor Carolyn Duggins is a woman of God who loves the Lord and has a heart for His people of all ages. She is thankful for the gifts and talents entrusted to her. She is devoted to her call to ministry and intercessory prayer. Her life scriptures are:

Lamentations 3: 22-23 *"It is of the Lord's mercies that we are not consumed, because His compassions fail not: They are new every morning: great is thy faithfulness."*

2 Corinthians 15: 58 *"Therefore my beloved brethren, be steadfast, unmovable, always abounding in the word of the Lord, forasmuch as ye know that your labor is not in vain in the Lord".*

Rev. Dr. Mary H. Washam

Dr. Washam, who holds the title of Bishop, is Senior Pastor and Founder of Hope Christian Tabernacle in Philadelphia, PA, and New Beginnings Deliverance Tabernacle in Middletown, Connecticut. Dr. Washam received her Ph.D and master's in Religious Education from the United Bible College and Seminary in Orlando, Florida, and her bachelor's degree from Jameson Christian College in Philadelphia, Pennsylvania. She was also Dean of Hope Bible Institute extension of Eastern Bible Institute, Irvington New Jersey.

She holds the office of President of Aglow International Lighthouse N. E. Philadelphia, Pennsylvania. Dr. Washam facilitated the group and helps promote God's Kingdom to the communities in Philadelphia.

The Challenge, Purpose, Power & Victory In Our Prayers

She has served as Philadelphia Police Chaplain for more than 15 yrs. providing emotional, moral, and spiritual support to officers, staff and their families and community policing engagement regularly.

Dr. Washam serves as an Advisor to Harvest Time International Ministries. As advisor she has traveled throughout the U.S., and other locations such as Africa, Puerto Rico, Mexico.

She is Founder and Executive Director of Hope Matters, Inc. a community driven nonprofit organization devoted to bringing healing to persons who have been impacted mentally, socially, emotionally, and spiritually.

With 30 plus years of counseling, coaching, and mentoring in the capacity of human services, community outreach, I developed my coaching/counseling practice entitled- Building Better Relationships Together LLC. BBRT offers individuals an opportunity to be exposed to healing in their lives in a safe professional atmosphere and environment. This process is a 3-step protocol program Trace- Erase- Replace that uses the concept of cognitive behavior.

Dr. Washam was featured in Triumphant Magazine 2023 Women of Worth for the month of March. She is the author of 3 published books:

- Does God Really Talk
- A Believer But...Do Believers Really Believe
- WAIT! 7 Checks B-4 I Do (relationship book)

Dr. Washam conducts professional writer's workshops, seminars, and retreats to help potential writers release their craft.

As a professional presenter and motivational speaker Dr. Washam is available upon request to address areas such as emotional, mental, social, financial, and spiritually related.

To connect with Dr. Mary Washam
Email: apolmhw@aol.com
Website: www.BBRT3.com
Phone: (215) 688-6012 or 1-(888) 444-1935 ext. 800

Rev. Gwendolyn E. Wheeler

She has served in ministry for over 25 years and is one of the pastors of New Beginning Fellowship Church in Philadelphia, PA. She embraced Jesus Christ as her Savior when she was 14 and has remained faithful to Him. She attended Deliverance Evangelistic Church School and completed the required classes, earning a certificate of completion. Additionally, she participated in a class with Neighborhood Crusaders under the guidance of Reverend Melvin Floyd, where she also received a certificate of completion.

She graduated from New Beginning Bible Institute and Training Center, chartered by Kingsway Christian College and Theology Seminary, with a diploma in biblical studies. In 1991, she joined the New Beginning Fellowship Church as a member. Later, in 1996, she was ordained as an Elder to preach the Gospel of Jesus Christ. Eventually, she became the Assistant Pastor of the New Beginning Fellowship Church, and as of June 2017, she is now the Pastor.

Rev. Gwendolyn E. Wheeler possesses various gifts, such as singing, teaching Sidewalk Sunday School, and performing in plays. All glory be to God for the incredible things He has accomplished through her.

In Closing...

Dear Readers,

We would like to express our deepest gratitude to everyone for joining us on this incredible journey through the book "Voices of Grace." It has been our honor and privilege to share the wisdom, insight, and inspiration of five extraordinary ministers of the Gospel.

Throughout the pages of this book, we hope you have found solace in the comforting words, guidance in the powerful messages, and encouragement in the stories these ministers share. Our earnest desire was to bring you closer to our Heavenly Father's boundless love and grace.

As you turn the last page of this anthology, we want to remind you that the teachings within its chapters are not meant to be read and set aside merely but to be reflected upon and carried in your hearts. May the profound truths unveiled in these pages continue to guide and uplift your faith journey.

We want to extend our heartfelt appreciation to the five ministers who so graciously poured their hearts and souls into the creation of this book. Their unwavering dedication and commitment to sharing the Gospel have undoubtedly touched countless lives.

Lastly, thank you, the readers, for embarking on this transformative expedition with us. Your support, feedback, and presence have been instrumental in making this book a reality. We hope that this anthology has left an indelible mark on your life and will continue inspiring you to live out your faith passionately and purposefully.

Thank you for joining us on this remarkable journey of faith, and may the grace and love of our Lord Jesus Christ be with you always.

Sincerely,

Rev. Dr. Julia D. McKinley
Rev. Dr. Mary H. Washam
Pastor Carolyn Duggins
Pastor Arlene Delores Presley
Rev. Gwendolyn E. Wheeler